# Verge 2017

# Verge 2017

## Chimera

Edited by Bonnie Reid, Aisling Smith
and Gavin Yates

Monash University Publishing
Matheson Library and Information Services Building
40 Exhibition Walk
Monash University
Clayton, Victoria 3800, Australia
www.publishing.monash.edu

Monash University Publishing brings to the world publications which advance the best traditions of humane and enlightened thought.

Monash University Publishing titles pass through a rigorous process of independent peer review.

http://www.publishing.monash.edu/books/verge2017-9781925495997.html

Series: Verge

Design: Les Thomas

Cover image: Jesse Boyd-Reid

**National Library of Australia Cataloguing-in-Publication entry:**

| | |
|---|---|
| Title: | Verge 2017 : chimera / edited by Bonnie Reid, Aisling Smith, Gavin Yates. |
| ISBN: | 9781925495997 (paperback) |
| Subjects: | Creative writing--Fiction. |
| | Short stories, Australian. |
| | Short stories, English. |
| | Poetry--21st century. |
| | Poetry, Modern--21st century. |
| | Chimera (Greek mythology). |
| Other Creators/Contributors: | |
| | Reid, Bonnie, editor. |
| | Smith, Aisling, editor. |
| | Yates, Gavin, editor. |

Printed in Australia by Griffin Press an Accredited ISO AS/NZS 14001:2004 Environmental Management System printer.

The paper this book is printed on is certified against the Forest Stewardship Council ® Standards. Griffin Press holds FSC chain of custody certification SGS-COC-005088. FSC promotes environmentally responsible, socially beneficial and economically viable management of the world's forests.

# Contents

# Foreword

This year's theme, Chimera, was born from a desire to transcend the mundane. In a world that sometimes feels like it's coming apart at the seams, we wanted to create something poetic and beautiful.

By no means is Chimera a retreat to the ivory tower. It confronts the evocation of desire: a journey seeking the essence of what is felt but not known. We wanted Chimera to urge contributors to search for a glimpse of this reality; it may lie just out of reach but its tenebrous presence is undeniable. We consider writing the Chimera an attempt to crystalise the beast—to witness the moment, before disappearing like a mirage.

As a trio, we loved its ambiguity and many layered meanings; the word is a semantic melting-pot. It unites the scientific with the imaginative. With its literary heritage from Homer, the monstrous, the mythical and the magical all come together.

The submissions we received responded to the theme in unexpected and original ways, and the pieces you are about to read delighted us with their creativity. These authors will transport, challenge and enthral you. Their settings will carry you across the world, and into different realms—from the individual's struggle with the corporatist leviathan to Fijian beaches, from the Australian outback to the monotony of suburbia. The characters struggle with dead-end jobs, lost children, absent parents and failed lovers. You will find poetry, fiction and one personal essay in the collection.

We are also extremely proud to feature three works associated with the 2017 Monash Undergraduate Prize for Creative Writing, for which the Judges gave a joint award this year. Aimee-Jane Anderson-O'Connor's 'Femina' is a beautifully executed tale of timelessness, with an experimental form. This story shares the prize with 'The Lady Who Walks' by Ann Jackson, a poignant exploration of family dynamics, the fragility of the mind, and multi-cultural experience of Australia. The highest placed Monash University student is Lauren Burridge whose story 'Glass' is one of love and loss.

In addition to this we gave two awards of our own. The *Verge* poetry prize was awarded to Joan Fleming's 'Allowances' for its raw power and syntactic ingenuity. We were immediately struck by the precision of this poem. The *Verge* prose prize went to 'Polyethylene Evergreen' by Killian Donohoe for its damningly sharp portrait of office life in the five-day workweek grind, carried over with deft narrative structure and comic relief. While these two pieces stood out for us, we are delighted by the quality writing that makes up the entire collection.

Much like the mythical Chimera itself, this year's *Verge* is a composite of many different things. And we are proud of an end result that we feel is something beautiful.

We hope that Chimera takes you on a journey of your own.

# Acknowledgements

The editors of Verge would like to acknowledge that this publication was created on stolen land of the Kulin Nations. We pay our respect to Elders past and present, with deep gratitude that we were able to publish and share these stories here.

Our thanks and appreciation, for making this publication possible, goes to:

Dr Ali Alizadeh, *Verge* Coordinator
Ali has been a tremendous support to the editorial team throughout the production. We have been lucky to have his generous guidance and wise words in putting together a great collection.
Dr Melinda Harvey, Melbourne Writers Festival and Emerging Writers Festival Liaison
Prof Robin Gerster, Director of the Literary and Cultural Studies Graduate Program
Dr Nathan Hollier, Monash University Publishing
Joanne Mullins, Monash University Publishing
Laura McNicol Smith, Monash University Publishing
Les Thomas, Monash University Publishing
Lisa Dempster, Melbourne Writers Festival
Sally Riley, Monash University

We would like to extend our gratitude to the following, who reviewed and critically appraised the pieces:

Dr Ali Alizadeh
Dr Cassandra Atherton
Dr Bonny Cassidy
Dr Stuart Cooke
Dr Elin-Maria Evangelista
Dr Gabriel Garcia-Ochoa
Dr Melinda Harvey
Dr Anthony Lawrence
Associate Professor Chandani Lokuge
Dr Rosalind McFarlane

Dr Alyson Miller
Dr David Musgrave
Dr Lucy Neave
Dr Catherine Noske
Dr Kay Rozynski
Dr Ariella Van Luyn
Dr Chris Watkin
Dr Jessica Wilkinson

We, and the contributors, give warmest thanks for your time and expert feedback.

Special thanks must also go to:

Phoebe Reid for her graphic design work on *Verge*'s publicity and cover design.

Jesse Boyd-Reid for the use of his photographs for *Verge*'s publicity and cover design.

And, most importantly:

The contributors.

It has been our pleasure to work with such talent: thank you for your dedication, and for sharing your journey through creative practice.

1

# in-flight movie

## *Jack Kelly*

whenever a character in a movie interacts with another
movie themselves it always seems to be a metaphor:
emerging drug-addict records echidna documentary,
love-sick millennial pirates HD Mature Vixen erotica,
*I'm Feeling Lucky* Google search returns three YouTube
videos of extraterrestrial contact— but for now just enjoy
the inflight movie about a mathematician who leaves
his job & hikes Mt Kosciusko in search of the asymptote.

2

# The Lemon Tree

## *Chloe Riley*

The tree was dead.

Its branches were naked, their brown colour faded to a dull grey. It hadn't borne fruit in over a year. I remembered how the last lot of lemons had simply dropped to the ground, freckled and rotten. Dad crouched by its roots and marked out the earth around it. The fresh grass cut away as he pressed through it with the tip of a little spade.

'That's the problem with fruit trees,' Dad told me. 'They're prone to disease, especially here. The environment's not right for them.'

'This block used to be an orchard.'

'Climate change,' he explained. 'I'm sure it made a great orchard once. But unless the weather settles, I doubt we'll see many fruit trees growing here again.'

I'd never really liked the tree. I didn't like lemons. They're sour. It was Nonno who'd done the landscaping for the house, before he died. At the centre, he'd put a large square patch of grass—a classic Aussie backyard in the middle of an Italian *giardino*. We were only half Italian, Mum's side. But living with Nonna was a constant reminder of our heritage.

It was Nonno who had planted the tree. He was from Vizini, but my Nonna had grown up on an orchard in Floridia. She'd had hundreds of trees exactly like it. Nonno probably planted it for her.

I came into the kitchen to make coffee. The caffettiera was sitting empty on the stove from this morning. Pulling it apart, I took out the filter. It was still full from the last pot. I struck it against the rim of the bin, watching the ashy remains fall limply into the bag.

I got two cups from the cupboard. Noticing the thick dark rings inside them, I realised Nonna had washed the dishes again. I hurried through the remaining cups, trying to decipher which were clean and which were dirty. Frustrated, I brought them all to the sink and turned on the hot water. The bottle of detergent was sitting unopened next to the tap. It was probably the only thing in the whole kitchen her greasy hands had not touched.

'*Devi usare il detergente!*'

I would tell her this time and time again, and she still wouldn't listen.

'Eh, *fai fatti tuoi!*'

We would often argue like this for half an hour, which would always leave a strange sour taste in my mouth. There had been a time when she would never have left a speck of dirt uncleaned.

The lounge room had once been the pride of Nonna's house. It was the mandatory room in every Mediterranean home, where the antique furniture, the 'family jewels' rather, were proudly displayed. The sofas were baroquely ornamented and cushioned in a rich maroon. The walls were neatly lined with fading photographs. Old photos of weddings and babies, but none of the lifetimes that had followed. There was another table covered entirely with broken frames of all the people in our family who had passed away— Nonna's private collection.

It was only the small flat screen TV that brought the room back to the twenty-first century. It was also probably the cheapest thing in the room, and definitely the only thing that worked. Not even the dusty chandelier had been rewired, and its switch was taped over to avoid causing a power outage. At night, the room would only be lit by the little TV.

I found Nonna sitting in front of it when I came in with her coffee. I'd also cut up some leftover panettone. It was a bit dry, but still good.

'*Beatrice?*'

It was what she always called me. Chloe was too hard for Italians to say, so Mum had ensured that I had a more suitable middle name. I was named after the woman Dante loved. He never told her though. He just loved her from afar.

'*Vuoi un po' di caffè?*'

I always liked how Italian felt in my mouth. My grammar was terrible and I could never remember enough vocabulary, but I could always pronounce everything right. She nodded in response and I placed the panettone on her lap and handed her the small cup. She clutched it gingerly in two hands and began to drink. I placed my own cup on the table and sat down on the arm of her chair. She was watching *My Fair Lady*.

'*Ti piace questo film?*'

Nonna waved a hand. 'Ah, I see many time. *Lei è pazza.*'

I smiled, glad she was in a good mood.

'Where is-a your mother?'

She'd already asked me this twice that day.

'At work, *l'ho detto prima.*'

She sipped her coffee contently, her thickly rimmed glasses reflecting the light of the screen. At ninety-two, she had outlived all her siblings and her small circle of friends. Every morning she would pray a rosary to her husband Giuseppe—my brother's middle name. At any other time of day she wouldn't think about her husband, just of her mother. Sometimes she would think Mum was *her* mother, or her sister. We let her think that. We let her think lots of things.

We sat for a while, the film playing in front of us unchanged in any way. She always laughed at all the same moments exactly the same way. I think I'd seen it more times with her than with anyone else. Her moments might as well have been a part of the film.

Audrey Hepburn sat singing on a vegetable cart, a bouquet of celery in her arms. I turned again to Nonna who was now munching on the aging panettone. She was wearing the same clothes she'd worn the past three days, now with an additional coffee stain on the collar. Normally I would have had a go at her about it; but looking at her sitting there, something stopped me. She was the quietest I had seen her in months. Her good days were quickly growing scarce and it was hard to remember when the last one had been. Her hand shook as the cake crumbled between her fingers and mouth, falling onto her blouse and skirt. I suddenly thought of the lemon tree in the back yard.

'*Ti ricordi l'albero di limoni?*'

'*Come?*'

'The lemon tree.'

She looked at me.

'*Che dici?*'

'Never mind.'

She returned to her coffee, her eyes fixed on the screen. I took in her crooked fingers, swimming under the weight of her sagging skin. Her gold band hung limply round her wedding finger. She'd lost weight again. She always forgot to eat if no one was home. She'd just sit there, shrinking away beneath her own skin. I tried not to think about this as I sat by her, watching Audrey Hepburn graciously transform from a cockney flower girl into a grand duchess.

'*Beatrice?*'

I looked at her. She placed one of her trembling hands on my arm.

'Where is-a your mother?'

Mum finally came home from work, slumping her satchel and laptop bag onto the table. She was in a bad mood. I came into the kitchen, just as she started storming about, fussing over dinner.

'I asked you to thaw the chicken.'

'No you didn't.'

'Check your phone.'

One missed call.

'Mum, you know I don't check voicemail.'

'Well you need to.'

She pulled the freezer drawer open and began to dig for the meat.

'Did Dad start on the tree?'

I remembered watching him scratching that thick ring through the grass. 'Yes.'

'Good, I've got someone coming for it tomorrow.'

I looked at her, bewildered. 'Tomorrow?'

She pulled out the meat and slammed the drawer closed.

'So soon.'

'Well it's just standing there, taking up space.' She looked up, finally seeing my face. 'I thought you hated it.'

I didn't answer.

She came to the sink, dropping in the meat and turning on the tap. She rubbed her fingers under the stream and began to prod its icy surface.

'It feels weird, getting rid of it.'

'Of what?'

'The tree.'

'Well it's dead.' She turned off the tap. 'You want a dead tree just standing in the backyard?'

'No.'

'Well?'

Again I said nothing.

Mum looked down at the meat. It was still frozen. She picked it up and began to whack it against the sink.

The workers came, just as she said. They came out of a truck, which was branded with a giant logo of a luscious tree in a neat circle. They all wore the same yellow polo—the image of the tree stitched clumsily on the left breast.

I watched them as they unearthed the tree. Its branches shook and I had a vivid image of how many lemons it had dropped in its lifetime. Perfectly good lemons that we had never even bothered to pick up. The men worked around the tree until they'd forged a moat. I looked into it, seeing for the first time the tree's thick roots, naked of soil. I turned around, not wanting to watch anymore.

I walked back to the house, trying to block out the sound. The thwack of shovels against the rock hard earth.

3

# Allowances

## Haasts Bluff sports weekend

### *Joan Fleming*

WINNER OF THE VERGE PRIZE FOR POETRY

Knows can be softer. Yellows might still dictate a green word. Books can be filthied and stillread. Little dogs can be stolen and are. Can be tyre bumped and are. Can belong and so there will be sorry, or can be a nothing dog. Camp cup can be all grime, surpassingly grime. Late dust light of the football kicked can be glamour, arc. Eyesoft in desert light can be. Good food can be with chicken salt. Opal petrol can be billboard declared THE LOW AROMATIC CHOICE. Clinic can look closed and have someone cool inside by a manual, asking those questions. Outside, the only white moon for miles is your face, here because *you coming?* and *Don't drink that water you get sore guts.* Palms can turn black; should. Bed can be borderfree and smell is travelling.

4

# Don't Touch the Billabong

## *Callum Methven*

When the lights flash red and blue
kids split like rotten fruit once more
another generation stolen,
falling through the same machine
whose fingers clutch the winning hand.
You said to close the gap
before the draught blows through
it's cold outside, you told me
throw the billy out with the water,
when the storm was over you asked me
is it summer this far south.

Waiting on the corner when the curtains draw
you see men and women
wearing blindfolds, fill the streets
with empty taxis and you grasp:
no one minds the spectre of the cloth.
Bedtime stories drown the din
of crying kettles and such things
as footfalls wake the dying
from their slumber. I've never seen
a mother fall so hard, but harder still it is
to make a grown man say sorry.

The black line stretches
from coast to coast, she casts no shadow.

None but the one that stalks us still
until we make it to the edge of the frontier.
This statue's hat is heavy like his spade
our buried memories rot like bodies in the sun,
and when the war was over you asked me
is it winter this far north.

By the by I saw a girl
she had an older woman's eyes,
she blew the candles out and made a wish:
to wish upon a seven-pointed star.
She was happy in her dreams
before we came and kicked the castle,
before she realised that
lesser ghosts than you and I
have haunted better men.

Waltzing through a hole in the ground
their stone lungs sigh ghosts of gold,
their haunting strikes it rich and so we sing:
but none can hear eureka in the dark.
If he were to strike it rich
it would not quell the hunger,
for the hunger only lives beneath the skin:
we tied a cape around our necks, we missed the mark.

By the by I saw a skeleton so small
it rattled around in my skull forever,
and skulls are bones, are puppets in a gale
and when the gale is done the smell persists:
well tell the kids don't touch the billabong.
The river runs a race that none of us can win
and when we lose the fish will swim upstream
amongst the dead, so spread the word:
don't drink the water from the billabong.
If forgetting is the remedy for troubled sleep
then to remember is a sip of toxic water,
so tell the kids don't touch the billabong:
you get too close, you just might see yourself.

5

# Femina

*Aimee-Jane Anderson-O'Connor*

## JOINT WINNER OF THE MONASH UNDERGRADUATE PRIZE FOR CREATIVE WRITING

### O

It is 1968 at Middlemore hospital. McCartney hums blackbird from anti-septic speakers and the woman pushes deep scarlet. There is no diamond in this shot. Only the cool clang of steel. Please hold your applause. The woman turns from white gloves and curls up woodlouse. Her mother holds the squirming babe. Exit doctor. Nurse. There is no spotlight for our protagonist. No curtain call. Yet here she is: Eve. Chalk and sheer slick, six pounds of nothing to see here.

### BC

Eve hangs asunder in the hot sun. Ripped and torn and bleeding, his mouth is filled with blood and vinegar. His head is laced with rusted thorns and he looks to the sky and enquires:

'Couldn't you have slipped me something to take the edge off?'

An albatross circles overhead, opens its beak and lo! The voice of Morgan Freeman echoes:

'I could have, but the people like to see their heroes suffer. The Book sales would have lagged. My good man, hang tight and think of the profit margin!'

# VIII

I want you to imagine it all sepia and worn at the edges. I want you to imagine the give of paper under the blue swill of a date, seven-something. Let's say six. Six has a nice sizzle. An orange leather armchair and brown pile carpet, brown like chocolate milk snorted good and thick. The kids congregate in a DEAD END and play cricket. Streets a-stick with tar, soles black and hard. Eve feels the saltwater bite of the bat. Stares blue and freckled at the mouthy boy with the backward baseball cap. He cracks his knuckles all impressive. Rubs the grapefruit against his camo leg and draws back. Eve flexes. Thwacks. The ball shatters citrus spray, lands guts first in the prickle grass. Eve runs piston while the others scramble for the pieces.

# X

The girls sit in a circle on the field. Pick daisies and worship the sun. Press buttercups to each other's faces and whisper secrets in the bathrooms. They practice kissing down by the creek, their lips pink and fourteen. These kisses are illicit. Subzero. Strawberry hushed. They will not tell their mothers. They will not tell their husbands.

# -1

Eve's belly is a pomegranate.
Its pips stir in the red dawn.
She has always known this is how it's gotta be.

# XII

The word virgin runs through the cathedral like a cold pulse. Sin began with the reaching hand, the soft tongue, wet lips. In the cathedral Eve learns to hold her body at arm's length. In the cathedral she is taught to love on her knees.

# 1969, Dunedin

Eve steps out from the craft and her boots grip the steps. The ground glows yellow like a hot bulb. Ochre dust swirls around her boots and the cameras flicker grey. It smells like spent gunpowder. She looks at it all, pocked and muffled quiet. She plants the Southern Cross and it flutters in the fan draught. She craves a cigarette. Sighs. The director clicks his fingers. She steps down heavy, slow—like they practiced. One small step for—man, one giant leap for—mankind. They will edit her baritone for the broadcast.

## XIV

In fourth form they are dragged into the school hall. 500 of them plaid and regulation, they shuffle in their plastic chairs. Some guest speaker from Auckland clears his throat and tells them that he is there to teach them self-defence. He has khaki shorts and calves like twisted straw. They watch his leg hair stop at the top of his socks.

They are told that one in four women will be sexually assaulted in her lifetime.

They look around the room and try to figure out who it will be. Her, with her hair wisping around her cheeks. Her with the home-stitched skirt and scuffed cuffs. Her with the cherry lipbalm. She leans too far over the water fountain. Opens her mouth too wide. Seems to enjoy the drink. The girls place chewing gum bets in the lunch hour. They rank themselves on a scale of one to four.

## XV

*Bloody* is a swear word in Eve's house and the kids whisper it while upstairs her sister traces *sharp* across her thigh. The word *thigh* sounds like vomiting in the backyard after six kilometres of somewhere else, she calls it *running*. All edges and hollow, Eve calls this *fit*. Eve spreads the potato across her plate like wet paint *and she does not call this anything*.

## XVI

Eve is packed into the back of the only Sunday bus. They lumber on the open road, past the toitoi and rabbit warrens. Past cream foam spray. The bus has no air-conditioning and the windows are welded shut with scratched globs of aluminium. Eve is wedged glass to knee with the woman beside her. She smells like cinnamon and orange kitchen cleaner. Clasps The Sunday Star like a life ring. Eve is listening to Madonna on her Walkman. Crunching Granny Smith between fuchsia lips. They round the corner, wide. Hit the rumble line, hard. Eve stops chewing and feels the sweat between her knees. The tug in her stomach. Eyes wide, cheeks red, Eve leans her forehead against the vibrating glass. Outside, the surf pulses salt and the seagulls cry and hoop.

## XVII

Eve's sister comes home with her neck sucked blood clot. Eve presses it. She giggles. He was from Italy. Eve gets a tablespoon from the freezer. A woman in Christchurch became partially paralysed after a clot from a hickey detached and travelled to her brain. She tells Eve about how his hair was thick and coarse as a pot scrubber. She drinks tequila dregs from abandoned shot glasses and asks Eve if she's given it up yet. Eve drinks Earl Grey and holds her hair back until dawn.

## Genesis 3:20

Adam named his wife Eve, because she would become the mother of all the living. Eve said 'Maybe we could consider my identity as something beyond my assumed reproductive potential?' 'Oh.' said God 'You're one of those mouthy feminist types? Hot.'

## XVIII

Eve is sober and sad and in the front seat. The driver grins and tells her that she is beautiful and it is a shame that a girl like her is going home all on her lonesome. The dash ticks red at five dollars a kilometre and Eve clenches her jaw. Works hard to look relaxed in her seat. She laughs too loud and tells the driver that she noticed he's maybe taking her the long way home. He blinks sorta fast and his smile falls some.

— You're not drunk are you? He says, and she says:

— No, I'm not. Why? And he says:

— Oh, no, that's good thing, far too many girls in my taxi, too drunk. I wouldn't say they deserve it but …

Eve notices his voice thin and faking. His enunciation so smooth, so silken, so liquid just moments ago.

— Not you though, you're smart, I can tell. And pretty too, did I mention? Not like those brown girls I get in here. Eve shifts in her seat and faces him.

— What?

— I just meant—

Eve squints out the windscreen. She has a headache, but they're nearly back at her apartment.

— Do you have a boyfriend?

Eve feels her ribcage tighten.

— No.

— Oh, then are you going to an empty house? Eve watches his fingers, thick on the wheel. Eve lies.

— A house full of flatmates. Stayed up late to ask about the party. A big one.

She looks at his ID swaying off the rear view mirror. She tries to lock his face in her mind. His name. She holds her phone, dead in her hand.

## 451

Eve is dragged through the streets naked still thrashing quivering skin torn off with clam shells as the sun passed o'er the earth's mid-way line the equator vernal burnt carbon blood libel under the equinox boots of an angry mob she returns unto ash is the first woman tried as a witch that is:

Not tried at all.

## XIX

Eve walks behind a girl on her way home from the gym. Street lights leach dim orange in the dark. Green recycling bins vomit glass onto the road. Couches spill their stuffing on the pavement. The girl glances behind her every ten metres and clenches her house keys between her fingers. Her shoulders are squared and Eve can see her breath in the air, white hot. She strides double time, her heels clack through powerline buzz. Eve crosses the street and hurries to pass her. Smiles at her, small and sorry. The girl grimaces and stares at the ground. Breathes out. Loosens her grip. Eve hugs his sister when he gets home.

# 1:35 AM

Eve dreams that her teeth fall out into her hand and she throws them like confetti. She pulls at them in the dark. Milk molars soft in her gums, canines made for tearing, she smiles through ulcerate curdle. Sucks them in with one great breath and spits them at the walls.

# XX

Eve's mother does yoga and smokes a pack a day. Holiday Menthol, 30, her throat purrs in the West Coast sun. Eve's mother is lavender incense and the Rolling Stones. Tarot and maypole. Athena. Aphrodite. Diana. Eve's mother is a nudist. She lives in a bell tent stacked with books and tobacco. Eve visits her twice a year. The club is littered with cherry blossom and tui. Gravel lines the drive. Caravans hum in a lazy O. Eve's mother has renaissance thighs and hips made for dancing. Eve has too much skin. The neighbours are caramel, butterscotch, soft and warm. The man next door stomps about in a white Sydney Zoo T-Shirt and nothing else. Eve's mother says that his back is scored grey with cancer, great chunks wormed out in the early stages. He kneels in the garden with a trowel and his penis hangs there. Flaccid, like some deflated Christmas yam. Eve hides in her pup tent. Slinks into the hot tub at midnight. She glows lunar. Caviar bubbles hook on her arm hair and she brushes them off with her fingertips. They float to the surface and burst.

6

# gordons bay

*Bonnie Reid*

assorted meat cuts laid out on sandstone bbq marinated in salt water every 20-30 returned to sun fading tattoos skin redder angrier by the minute too loose black swimwear framing bodies more masc. esp. adidas all varieties of body hair and body hair removal that help you to present yourself accurately in the club on the beach when you're walking the king st runway kinda stretches more through enmore to marrickville these days wondering do all the stingrays manta-rays whatever-rays see all the bods on the rocks from their camouflage on the sandy-bottomed bay and know they're at unofficial queer beach cruising spot scene to be seen? maybe a bunch of underwater queens all here for the same thing get a look at the stinger on him! you keep hearing it in your head that line 'it was just in me to be liking females' so many problems with this phrasing also it is perfect just right makes you open to all the babes in this human rookery came here with the queen of queers top down in the red capri took a shortcut from the car park wasn't really a shortcut now you're bleeding in stripes sport fashun elbow to knee 'that looks fuckin' gnarly dude' says c who is of course here too 'yeah fell down a cliff' cliff means 2 metre brick wall but you got a lot of bravado to knock out between you coz you fucked once don't talk about it just shows how cool chill super chiller you are almost like you could do it again you won't maybe you will probably it's not a good idea still bleeding find shaded rocks see ten other queers you know try not to bleed on them too see k he is flashing his glitter nails at you share your theory of glitter with him at any given time everyone on earth has a piece of glitter somewhere on or inside them there is probably glitter in space dust you bet glitter was shot into space with the astronauts or maybe it sucks off earth into space some kinda breeze pulling slowly how else do we keep moving further from each other while the population grows? 'glitter is space dust babe! i snorted glitter once and did a glitter shit' says k 'do you think it counts as glitter when it's inside you where no light gets in?' 'you're speaking for yourself babe the light shines outta me!' time for a dip before fish burgers drake and t swift on the way home to your life that's all yours and you don't know what you're doing with it

7

# Turner's Prize 45, XO

(A construct of hope and chromosomal anomalies

realised in a miscarriage)

*Kerryn Salter*

For years,
I've been signing off my name
with an 'xo'—
A kiss and a hug
from a someone, and a no one.

Bloated and bursting with
expectations and an imagined personification
of you,
I am left with nothing. Zero. An 'oh,
I am sorry.'
An o, where there should be an x.
Hollow sentiments,
instead of something I can put my arms around.

# She Watched a Lot of Television

## *Natalie Briggs*

She is a good boyfriend
Brings me a glass of water

We eat French toast, need each other

She asks me to watch her dance
I say *ask a dancer to watch you dance*

I buy pasta for us to share
We know it's a mistake
She walks back to the counter
Orders soup

I watch her throw meat at a sheet of plastic
For art
She has good form

Kneeling on her bathroom floor
No guard on the clippers
*This is concept porn,* she says
Hair on my clothes
Makes me take them off and shower

*Don't fall down the stairs*

She wouldn't let me watch her blow her nose
I would have liked to see what ever needed to come out of her
Come out of her

I finally sent the text
*I miss your mouth*
*Want to come over*

I tried the text out on a friend before I sent it
I used the pineapple emoji
There were no emojis in the final draft

At the reading she said *you are strong*
Asked me to kiss her cheek
The man she was sleeping with looked at us

You were good with my body
Held it

I don't hate you but I don't love you
I nothing you

I miss your teeth and laugh
That's all really
You stressed me out

You watched a lot of television
I watch *Friends* now

She wants to be Eileen Myles
I tell her
*Eileen Myles isn't even Eileen Myles*

I am taking time away from love
I am letting it go
My shoulder hurts I want to sleep alone

# Polyethylene Evergreen

*Killian Donohoe*

WINNER OF THE VERGE PRIZE FOR PROSE

Bob Geldof (the smug prick) and the Boomtown Rats (probably fine) were wrong. I don't mind Mondays. Wednesdays are hard work.

Monday and Tuesday, we ask how the weekend was. Thursday and Friday, we ask what's on for the weekend. But on Wednesday we're unmoored and adrift—one weekend receded too far behind, the other impossibly far off— and there is nothing to talk about. Our disinterest is like an open fly.

Hump day, am I right?

Fuck me.

\*\*\*

On Friday mornings Marianne comes around our division with a lunchbox and an iPad. The lunchbox is for voluntary gold coin donations and the iPad is to record who's given what.

She will come up behind my desk, chewing gum like it's a chore, announcing her arrival with a rattle of the lunchbox. Every week I give her a pageant smile and ask how she is on this magical Friday morning and which segment of the community we're enriching this week. Every week she rattles the lunchbox again and motions to the masking tape label with her big block letters indicating the lucky recipients of 236 dollars in gold coins.

Ask her another question and the children or the whales or whoever will go without your two bucks.

***

Once a month your Friday gold coin donation buys you the privilege of wearing casual clothes. Yeah, the same deal they ran on the last day of term when you were at primary school. On casual Fridays, the black R.M. Williams turn to brown, the collars soften and a diverse ecosystem of little animals from the zoo of the well-to-do sit stitched on our hearts.

If you were to ask what the 'work/life balance' slapped across the front page of their website means (which you wouldn't), they'd probably talk about casual Friday. The work component is represented by the work that you have to do like any other day, and the life component is represented by the Christmas-present-from-Nan polo shirt that you only wear at work once a month.

***

Every second Friday night there are drinks in the boardroom from 4:30, where, fortified by clean skin wines and original flavour chips, we show face and barely feign interest in each other's chat.

Geoff, a recently divorced partner, will try to bond with me over an assumed shared appreciation of the size of a coworker's boobs (bloody massive, by his estimation).

Leanne will work the room like a great politician, entering conversations naturally, adding something funny or interesting and then moving on soon after. It took me a while to realise that between most of her moves she'll swing past the boardroom table, filling her wine glass so it's never less than half-full.

Hugh or someone like him will tell me about the theoretical bump in the value of the house he bought six months ago, which he'll most likely die in. I'll ask if his dick has grown proportionally with his return on investment, or some other half-joke, naked in my jealousy. Because what else are any of us really here for, if not to reach and then remain at that quaint old marker of Australian adulthood: Home Ownership.

When the drinks run out, those remaining—usually without friend or imagination—will wander to a nearby pub to continue the bonding.

We'll end up at one of the standard Friday night pubs, with artfully exposed light bulbs, a marble bar and a great selection of craft beers. Prior to the change in management and subsequent refurbishment, these were the sorts of pubs where broken old men would piss themselves on their stools with sad frequency.

In half-shouted conversations I'll bond with girls over our shared experiences working for financial behemoths. If all goes well I'll have fairly satisfying sex in the missionary position with a girl called Steph, Soph or Bec. A quick scan of my LinkedIn profile the next day will reveal that I'm not an investment banker.

\*\*\*

The non-stop thrill ride of Fridays aside, there are four other days prior to push through. In those days you look to whichever higher power you covet most, be it Jesus, drink or prescription meds.

Philip is my work Jesus.

He doesn't attend work social events. He rarely speaks to anyone. He eats a rotating lunch of McDonalds, KFC, Nandos or Hungry Jacks alone in his office every day, with industrial metal music scraping out of his tinny computer speakers. And on each and every casual Friday, he wears a different Hawaiian shirt coupled with a pair of slacks and white New Balance walking shoes. He's 29.

Committed by almost anyone else, such acts of rank subversion would be considered a terrorist threat to the vaunted corporate culture and punishable by interminable HR 'catch-ups,' and possibly even being sent down for re-education on 'what we stand for.' But Philip—and it's Philip, not fucking Phil—is near unimpeachable by virtue of his beautiful gift for ugly work.

Should you, by divine gift or by your own design, have cause to go to his office, he won't acknowledge you until he reaches a natural end to the stanza of the balance sheet he's currently working on. Only then will he look up from his three monitor set-up (standard issue is two). But in those gorgeous moments between entry and acknowledgment, you are in an audience of one with a maestro at the height of his powers. Fingers fly and data dances. The hands move with the ferocious precision of an expert lover. I imagine a fine film of dust on his delete key—its existence a wry joke between the good people of Hewlett Packard and the accounting gods.

He does this all day. Then at 5:15, he leaves and the rest of us don't.

To be clear, I have little to no adulation to spare for accountants or accounting as a species and a dark art, respectively. But Philip, whether he cares to think about it or not, is one of the very few in this place whose proficiency for the work allows him to sell it alone. He trades his labour and not so much as a smile more.

Those of us, most of us, possessed of lesser talents are forced to throw in various added extras to retain the privilege of bathing in the halogen glow for 60 hours a week. We show up to networking events, ask after the family and agree to participate in corporate triathlons alongside hundreds of old suits that lycra was simply not intended for.

So I suppose woe is me, the financial proletariat, doing wrist straining work day in, day out for a bit less than 100k a year. But then again, if an accountant doesn't have at least some claim to existentialism, who the fuck does?

***

Inspired by Philip's conscientious objection from all but the specific dictates of his contract, but not quite good enough at my job to do the same, I devise my own white collar rebellion.

We work on the upper floors of a glass tower you've seen but wouldn't recognise. The temperature is room temperature, never rising or falling from 20 degrees Celsius. The tinted windows prevent the sun from disturbing the white neon light I used to only know from the dentist's chair. The little bin next to my desk is always empty when I arrive in the morning, the disposable coffee cup and few stray post-it notes I put in there yesterday disappear overnight. We will be here forever, consistent in light, temperature and considered financial judgment.

The only sign of life beyond Phillip's Hawaiian metal parties is the big potted tree at the end of the reception desk in the lobby. But then that too, is plastic—a more reliable form of life.

Each evening after the receptionists have left for the day, I pass through the lobby, yank a handful of leaves from alternating parts of the tree, pocket them and leave.

I chip away from the trunk outward, maintaining an even level of surface foliage and gutting the inside. After four months of disciplined pruning, all that remains is the outer facade of leaves.

Look, Rosa Parks I am not. But it's a worthy physical reminder of a truth excluded—that real life is barred from this place as much as death. And if that vaguely pathetic little claim to honesty lets me stay here, then so be it, because I can't play guitar and I'm far too precious for manual labour.

I don't know where else to go.

\*\*\*

I work late on a Thursday, after a day of conspicuous complaints about how flat chat I am.

At about 11:00, when I'm confident I'm the last one here, I get a beer from the fridge on the meeting room floor and head to the lobby. I take a second to behold the leaf facade I've engineered, perfectly hollow beneath a lush outer layer. I briefly wonder how much an arborist makes, before setting upon the tree to finish the job.

After months of considered pruning there's a satisfying crudeness in ripping fistful after fistful from the tree, exposing the plastic branches beneath. I fill a plastic shopping bag with the leaves and it's done.

I sit on the leather and foam block they call a couch and take in the scene while I finish my beer.

It's all white marble, black leather and stainless steel, angular and oppressively bright, as though the pearly gates were actually in a stockbroker's loft in downtown New York. And at the end of the marble slab reception desk is a massive matte black pot holding up the thin brown skeleton of a plastic tree that couldn't survive here.

\*\*\*

I get to work at 7:30 the next day to get another look at my handiwork and hopefully catch some of the early birds in their confusion, disgust or, more likely, disinterest.

What I find is a lush plastic tree in a massive matte black pot.

\*\*\*

That night I bury my hand inside the tree, break off a handful of leaves, pocket them and leave.

# 10

# toothpaste

## *Jack Kelly*

ingredients absorb into the stomach  money falls into the meter
coke falls out of the vending machine  how do you make coke
what are you doing  read the instructions  the machine won't begin
don't believe in electricians  have the first sip  how does it taste
you don't need the recipe  enjoy the food on your plate
don't clear up the mess  leave the scraps  the dog will eat it
don't think about it  you are excused  get some fresh air  sit down
take a sip of coke  brush your teeth  a dirty doormat
the door is open  don't press the doorbell  no one can hear you
dirty teeth  there is only peppermint ice-cream  the meal is over

# The Sexton's Apprentice

## *Jena Woodhouse*

The carpenter arrived in a deluge,
sent by a friend to replace a step.
Waiting beneath the eaves for the rain
to ease, he said he'd dug graves
in Bucharest ~ fresh from the village
in wolfish times, glad of a place
to lay his head, a crust of bread,
a secluded space to wield his spade
and commune with the dead.

The dead, he claimed, cling to the hope
that the living cherish their memory.
He'd often heard them sigh as they sucked
the scent from funeral wreaths.
Flowers on graves were robbed of fragrance,
such was the craving of the deceased,
but enterprising gypsy boys
would steal the stale blooms, nonetheless.
Once, unaware, he'd bought their lilies
for a girl he hoped to impress,
who flung the white flutes in his face.
*The dead have drained the scent!* she said.

Drenched, the sexton fixed the step
then vanished, wordless as a wraith.
But for the tread he'd replaced,
I might have doubted we had met.
Perhaps the jasmine-scented rain
reminded him of Bucharest.

# 12

# Umbra

## *Gavin Yates*

Umbra. Cathedral rain in arms:
in come the mountains, thin
as wallpaper. That elsewhere,
foot in the flickering: white navel
against the seams. Among the other
places, you walk on the table.

    Approaching this,
to unhinge the face of moths—
then disperse. That those were lost
fingers wandering keys: I put
my phone and wallet to the side.

# 13

# Saudade

*Aisling Smith*

It was Beatriz who apologised for both of them.

'Sorry we're late,' she said in her pretty, accented English. Jack felt the rosacea of embarrassment on his cheeks—at one stage his Portuguese had been good enough for her not to have to switch.

Her friends had obviously been seated at the table for a while; the water glasses looked like they had been emptied and refilled several times, and the paper table cloth was creased. But they simply waved the apology away and stood to embrace the two latecomers—kisses on both cheeks for Beatriz and handshakes for Jack. They were as welcoming as ever and, forgetting for a moment, Jack wondered fleetingly why he'd left it so long to come back.

He clambered onto the low bench seat and Beatriz tucked in beside him. It wasn't really big enough for everyone and Beatriz and Jack were mashed together, thighs and shoulders pressed tight. The other faces around the table were unnervingly familiar to Jack. João and Tiago were the two men, and he recognised Carolina, Inês and Lúcia as well. João was quick to speak, his voice warm.

'Welcome back, my friend. It has been far too long.'

'It has. I've missed this place.'

They'd known each other pretty well three years ago, but that seemed so far away now. Still, everyone was smiling at him and when they spoke, they used English like Beatriz for his sake. Jack sat, feeling awkward in his monolingualism and uncertain whether it was okay to laugh when they made jokes about the Spanish.

The pacing waitress in her slinky black jumpsuit took their order for drinks. Jack asked for green wine, a speciality from around here which he felt a blossoming eagerness to taste again. The others ordered red.

'You're such a tourist,' Beatriz's cool voice murmured at his shoulder. Jack thought she sounded reproving rather than affectionate, but the others just laughed. Well, she was half-right—he was both a tourist and not. 'I'll order some food for us, shall I?' she added to him. She read the menu silently, her professionally manicured hands spreading it open, each finger capped by the pale sliver of French tips. It was only after she started working at the gallery that she started bothering with that bullshit. She wouldn't have cared three years ago. And Sarah back home certainly didn't.

'Beatriz tells us you're working as a lawyer now?' said João, offering tinder for small-talk.

'Yeah,' Jack muttered. 'It's not too bad.'

He never knew what to say about the tiny law firm where he'd managed to score his first proper job. He chatted a bit about it and João was nodding, but with an expression of politeness rather than true interest. It was a relief when the waitress brought their drinks and the conversation was interrupted for a toast.

'Saúde!'

Jack placed the wine glass to his lips, thinking that he had never quite gotten used to the lack of reaction being a lawyer caused here—the Portuguese had been more interested when he'd simply been studying liberal arts. Certainly Beatriz had never understood why he hadn't pursued studies in philosophy instead. At his elbow, she had turned pointedly away and was talking to the three girls. Jack didn't mind; they'd run out of things to say days ago. João and Tiago started to chat, still in English, but mostly to each other. The table had ripped right down the middle, two conversations forming, and Jack stuck between them, unsure of which one to follow. He sipped the green wine and, around them, the restaurant buzzed and hummed.

Three years ago, this place had been home. He'd lived with Beatriz in Porto for twelve months after university. He'd even been offered a place to do his Master's degree in philosophy in Lisboa—and had turned it down to go home and get a job in the law. In hindsight it seemed ludicrous and he'd spent the next two years waiting for a similar opportunity to come up again, but it never had. Yet at the time, he was missing Australia terribly, and long-distance had seemed easy and romantic: him and Beatriz separated by oceans and miles. Back then, he'd never felt love so intensely before; he scribbled poems for her in a notebook and spent his scholarship money on flowers for her room. He'd bought books in Portuguese and read through them laboriously with a dictionary, webbing them with marginalia. For her part, she'd painted tiny watercolours for him and brought home pastéis de Nata from the bakery, just because he liked them. And in Edinburgh she'd braved the weather to watch every single one of his rugby matches, shivering in the wind despite her scarf. He'd been convinced that they would be okay.

Yet when he left, Beatriz had been nervous.

'I feel *saudade*,' she had said when she dropped him off at Departures. Her accent had thickened as it always did when she was upset and her hands had flown upwards to articulate something she obviously couldn't voice. *Saudade*—she had never been able to really translate what the word meant. He'd looked it up, but the sterility of the dictionary's explanation and fussy etymology hadn't helped much. It hadn't let him *feel* the word. He thought perhaps that you had to be Portuguese to truly understand what it meant. At the time, he had assumed that she was simply saying she'd miss him and only later did he realise that there was far more packed into that elusive word. It was deeper, more ceaseless. The 'I'll miss you too,' he'd told her in return had not been anywhere near adequate—and when he'd eventually realised his mistake he had felt queasy with disappointment. *Saudade*: a collision of past, present and future. The deep chasm of loss for what has passed, which mingles with the hopeless longing for its return. The dregs of love which cause both melancholy and resignation. Not just a gap in the English vocabulary, but something that never existed in the first place.

Of course, in the early days he'd travelled back to Portugal as often as he could or she'd flown to Melbourne. But somewhere along the way their physical distance had led to a distance of another sort. They had busy existences in different countries—separate lives and new possibilities. The trips had petered out and the last time she had come to see him, a good six months ago, he knew he hadn't been attentive enough. He'd let himself get distracted by work and she'd been left to wander around town by herself. Sure, he'd taken her out in the evenings; they had sat across from one another in the newest, most expensive restaurants he'd been able to think of. The sheen on the moonstones around Beatriz's throat and hanging from her ears had been set to best advantage in the candlelight, but she'd mostly looked at her plate or out the window, rather than at him. The night she had to leave, he told her fervently that he loved her—clutched her body to him and whispered in her ear—and she'd murmured an agreement, but it was only when that bulky jet had carried her away, back to the Northern hemisphere that he'd *actually* felt longing for her settle back in his body. He'd called her on Skype and, looking at her face on the screen, had felt closer to her than he ever had when she'd been visiting. He commented on this to Sarah at work and she'd scrunched her nose thoughtfully.

'You only want her when she isn't around,' she diagnosed.

'You're a bloody solicitor not a shrink, what the hell would you know?' Jack had laughed.

'I like the unavailable ones, too,' she'd answered, shrugging, and had given him a look which he'd been replaying in his mind ever since.

But this trip to Porto was one that had been planned for a while: he and Beatriz were celebrating five years together. He'd already booked tickets last year and bought her a white-gold bracelet. And, after all, she had told him how excited she was for him to arrive.

But for the first time ever, Beatriz hadn't picked him up from the airport. It was a late flight and he'd asked her not to, but he had found himself scanning the crowd for her anyway. As he'd waited at baggage claim, his mind had offered him sly images of her expectant face on the other side—of course! She would have planned to *surprise* him. *You told her not to come*, he reminded himself, but his lips were already curving upwards; they had convinced themselves that she would be there. He'd hauled the block of his suitcase off the carousel and the metal of the handle felt as cold as 38,000 feet and 17,746 kilometres as he gripped it. But as he'd trundled through that final security gate, the only faces on the other side were those of strangers. Bored tour guides holding name-cards or locals in little clusters craning to see their loved ones coming through behind him. The women here looked like her— petite, with long dark hair worn loose around their shoulders. But no Beatriz in sight.

Jack had taken a taxi instead, giving the directions to her flat—their flat— in his halting Portuguese. He'd studied Spanish at school and still sometimes had to fight the urge to say *gracias* instead of *obrigado*. Porto's streets had unspooled before him in cobbled undulations. Even in the street-lit darkness he could see the blue and green of the tile on every second townhouse. Despite having lived here, he had never quite gotten over the fading beauty of the place. The oceanic colours of the cracked tile would jolt him and he'd shake his head in wonder: *I am living in another country.* This from a boy who never thought he'd finish high school—the first in his family to get to university, the first to even live outside of Frankston. But now, driving past it in the flesh, he felt only a vague intellectual appreciation. *You're in fucking Porto*, he admonished himself, but the old excitement lay dormant.

The first time he'd visited, Beatriz had taken him to the glossier Lisboa first. He'd walked the sunlit streets with her, listened to *fado* at night and tasted *ginjinha*, with its bell-like name, its tintinnabulation. It was the sort of word he wanted to say over and over again, just for the pleasure of shaping those sounds. *Ginja, ginja, ginja*! But Porto was something else. The Dark City he'd once heard it called, for its pathways were medieval and splashed in shadows. Although the city's monuments were lit up at night in muted tungsten, there were great black patches between the streetlights. Yes, the city was darker and heavier than Lisboa, but Jack couldn't think of it as The Dark City. That betrayed the richness of its history, the grandeur of its many bridges and all its triangles of greenery. To Jack, Porto would only ever be colourful—the river twisting below the city and the fluttering flags of washed clothes draped from twine across most balconies, all bright and beckoning.

When the taxi had finally halted at the street corner in Foz, the driver pocketed the 20 euro note. On the pavement in his winter coat, Jack had looked up at the building where light shone from the sixth floor windows. The apartment belonged to Beatriz's parents, but they'd never lived there. It was a swanky kind of place, but Jack's shoes were too loud, too heavy on the marble, and his plaid shirt clashed. The cables of the elevator pulled him soundlessly upwards and he got off on the sixth floor, right in front of the apartment they'd shared. Should he ring the doorbell? Or let himself in with the key on his chain? He'd hesitated and then pressed the button.

Then the door was swinging backwards and there she was. Beatriz. She looked different. Older, maybe.

'Hola!' she smiled as she trilled her greeting and slipped close to him. Thin arms circling around his middle, his nose and lips pressing against the crown of her head where her scent was strongest. He'd never been able to place it: some milky sort of shampoo and clean skin. Here, away from the harsh pixilation of Skype she was suddenly real again—the living breathing girl he'd fallen in love with five years ago. Shouldn't that be better than a thumbnail on the screen? The familiarity of her face and all the tiny humanising flaws he had forgotten: her heavy eyebrows and the faint smile lines which already bracketed her mouth. She'd always felt to him like a puzzle piece falling into place, but now as he waited and expected that sensation to spread over him, he felt just as disconnected as he had standing outside the flat, staring at the front door.

'Hola,' he had replied and tried to kiss her just how he used to. But all he could feel was the residue of stale cabin air in his mouth and dusted over his skin.

Lost in thought, Jack was jolted back to reality when the oozing Francesinha sandwiches Beatriz had ordered for them arrived. The two of them started to eat, Jack scoffing the sauce with messy delight. Everyone else was starting their second glass of wine, while Jack was finishing his third—and scanning the room for the waitress to order a fourth. He drank more steadily and seriously than he did when they were at university and Beatriz looked annoyed.

'Don't you think you've had enough for now?' she whispered sharply in his ear and he felt the flush erupt over his face.

'I'm an Aussie,' he joked stoutly. 'We've never had enough.' But he knew his shoulders had stiffened. Beatriz was fiddling with the stem of her own wine glass and he thought again of how obnoxious those nails looked. Those ridiculous white crescents.

Jack knew that he was trying—more than she was. Even her body language was a barrier: she had half turned away, her back a narrow shield against him as she chatted to the girls, but her leg still pressed up against him in their squeezed position. She was always composed. It wasn't something she was growing into with age, she'd been like that even when he first met her in a campus bar in Edinburgh. The others had been typical twenty year olds, doing shots of Stolichnaya and screeching their drunken revelry. Beatriz had sat with a glass of wine and thoughts that he could see but not interpret behind her eyes. It had been exhilarating trying to get to know her; each little fragment of her that he sifted to the surface had required effort and patience. And so he had eventually come to know the person behind the reserve. She was studying art history and languages. He had thought that he'd won her with his humour, but she told Jack later that she'd first started liking him when she realised he always spoke about his parents with respect. Family was important to Beatriz. In truth, she was more often the one to make him laugh with her dry wit.

But now she sat perfectly upright, not a vertebra out of place—and Jack thought that she had become stiff as whipped egg white. She'd been different at university . . . Or maybe he had been. He wished that she'd loosen up a little. A girl like Sarah would sprawl. When they occasionally went out for after work drinks, Sarah would sit with her left ankle on her right knee, and she threw back her head when she laughed.

'Your last night here?' said João, startling Jack. It wasn't really a question.

'I fly home tomorrow,' Jack agreed. He said the word *home* automatically and then paused, glanced over at Beatriz for her reaction, but her low voice was still in a flow of Portuguese with Carolina.

'Home.' It hadn't gone unnoticed by João and he sounded surprised. He exchanged a glance with Tiago. 'When are you coming back here?'

Jack hesitated.

'Soon,' he lied.

Both João and Tiago looked relieved. *You two are so lovely together*, everyone had always said. Jack and Beatriz were the success story—the exemplary couple, the iridescent aspiration. Wreathed in illusions.

The last time Jack had visited, he and Beatriz had happily sat arm in arm. The only thing he'd noticed about her nails was how good they felt stroking his skin, while Beatriz had laughed rather than jeered when he ordered an extra glass of green wine. And the last time they had had dinner with her five friends, the conversation had not splintered into little shards the way it had tonight. Denial was trying to cast its warm blanket over him once more, but Jack held it at bay and stood shivering in the shadows. What if he could no long measure Beatriz by decades or even years? One day not even this city of bridges and memories would help them span the chasm.

Realisation was thickening sourly inside him, curdling like dairy. Unanswerable questions coming unbidden from a voice he'd been trying to ignore all week: *but what now?* And the sudden premonition that one day he'd visit Porto for the last time. One day he would take the Lou Reed album he'd left in her CD holder and his old tartan scarf from the cupboard. *Together forever*, the solid gold aspiration of all young lovers and the dire lead weight which carried them down to drown. It bred complacency—and forever wasn't something to be complacent about.

'Look at you,' Tiago chuckled, gesturing at Jack and Beatriz sitting so close, unaware of how it was necessity rather than desire which kept them pressed together. 'Can't keep you two away from each other.'

But, for now, Jack just smiled and raised his glass to João and Tiago.

# 14

# Codral

## *Bonnie Reid*

The man wearing the white coat
asks you: 'Have you ever taken these
before?' 'Yes,' you say. 'Are you
pregnant?' he asks. 'No,' you say.
He looks hard at you. 'But is there
any chance you could be?' he insists.
Your neck prickles. You've had this
conversation too many times. You
say to the man: 'I want to give you
something to know.' But he hands
you the packet of pills. He says, 'Here,
take these pills.' Which is odd, you
think—his gesture already implying
this instruction. Maybe the man
thought he was giving you something to know. When you leave the
chemist you pop two of the pills out
of the silver packet. You look at them
in your palm. You imagine they are
the words of the man, ossified. You
swallow them with water. You drink
much more water than you need to
get them down. You bury them in
water.

# 15

# The Courteous Interlocutor

## *Megan Blake*

What you need to understand here, Rachel, is that you've missed the beautiful simplicity of feminism—of any egalitarian ideology, actually— because they're all just about joy. Pure joy. So with these ridiculous claims you make about 'objectification,' it's almost like the Second Wave didn't happen: that it didn't already liberate women from the moralising of other women. Or did I miss something, Rachel, and it's still the 1950s? From what Casey has said in all her interviews about the cover shoot, she did not have issues exercising her personal agency. Ergo, this is about her freely *choosing* to pose naked, as a decisive stroke in her own emancipation. The whole point of Second Wave feminism, Rachel, is that it is up to each and every woman to determine *for herself* what being strong and self-assertive means. If to Casey that means a revealing photo, then that is what must be hailed as her feminist triumph! She's a beautiful, successful woman. They're not breasts: they're symbols of proud, independent womanhood. And I don't know what you're attacking *me* for, when I am clearly on the side of women's rights: I am not the problem here. May I recommend you save your disgust for people who actually *are* sexist, because that's what we should be stamping out. The true misogynists—'The sexiest bitch ever.' I mean, really! These pricks are the problem. You know, I've always liked the title of that Anne Summers book, *Damned Whores and God's Police*. Do you know what that title means, Rachel? It means that, before Second Wave, women could either be whores or moralistic nay-sayers: those were the two options given to them. They could not be sexually assertive without also being trash. That idea was con- fronted in the 70s and, to my mind, defeated—over forty years ago! But now here you are, judging another woman as trash. No, no—yes, you are. You said you didn't care about her personal, individual freedom, and then you proceeded to judge her on the basis of her actions. Excuse me, Rachel, but—if I may say—criticising the actions a person chooses to perform is *not* different from criticising the person themselves; both leave the victim cowering under the spectre of judgment. And the argument that she gains some magical 'social capital' (that you have conveniently left unquantified) at the expense of others is disingenuous, because it pretends that social capital is a zero sum product—that any gained by one person must be at the cost of that held by others—and ignores the fact that the aim of the movement is, obviously, to advance the capital of all women simultaneously. So, *really*, it just tries (unsuccessfully, I might add) to obscure what is clearly your assumption: that it is your job to judge her for not being 'feminist' enough. She's pursuing her own legitimate self-interest, and have you considered the fact that maybe she's too busy to pay attention to your dictates regarding the modes of acceptable self-expression? Are you one of God's Police now, Rachel? Forty years ago we reached a point, thanks to your Second Wave sisters, where we moved *beyond* the labels of 'whore' and 'Madonna'—where women didn't have to be either sluts or God's Police, and they could be free to express their own sexuality without being subjected to your judgment. Every woman now has the right to choose whatever she wants for herself, without coercion from anyone, from any man, and no-one can stop her. What is so frustrating to me is that we finally get to a time and a place in history where every woman is free to choose her own destiny, her own happiness, her own definition of 'power,' how she personally wants to feel sexy and good about herself, and then you come along, dragging us back into the old days. And to think I was hoping to have an intelligent conversation on the topic! Instead, I got *you*. No, I never said it was meant to be an exhaustive summation of Second Wave feminism. No, no I didn't. And I think if you were paying attention to what I said you would know that, or perhaps you're just being wilfully ignorant. You might, I suppose, have simply misinterpreted what I said—and, for that, I apologise. It was obviously casual wording. But what I *said* was that Second Wave feminism was very much tied up with the liberation of women—especially the liberation of women from people like you—from the rules about what roles they were permitted to play in the complex discourse of sexual politics. So, you judging her behaviour as somehow 'not feminist' (as though that phrase has any meaning when the behaviour in question is something determined by her free choice) is casting her into the role you have defined for her as 'whore.' And you know what that makes you, Rachel? Now, I never said anything about being sexy to others— no, I didn't. No, I didn't, and please let me finish. I said, Rachel, that maybe she wants to feel sexy *for herself*, and maybe that's what *she* thinks is sexy. What you need to understand is that some women feel sexy by being seen as sexy in other people's eyes, and that's what is empowering for *them*. Showing that you're externally attractive doesn't have to be about winning the approval of others; even if it is, it's not your place to dictate to her the rules for what actions she feels *for herself* are self-affirming. As a man, I support Casey's desire to do whatever the heck she wants. I support the right of every woman to choose for herself what her values are, her standards of behaviour, her identity, the choices she wants to make and what feminism means to *her*. That's *my* version of feminism. *Her* version of feminism includes the right to pose for a risqué magazine cover without it being judged by anyone, man or woman. What I do *not* support is the regressive controls you're attempting to institute under the feminist label, denying her right to define it in a way that is meaningful for her, and shutting down free expression and choice in a way that, may I say, is entirely un-feminist. Are you denying the validity of either of those positions, Rachel? I can't imagine so. And, if not, what on earth are you here to argue for? The question I have for you is, are you not the least bit bothered by the intractable contradiction of your position, Rachel? Are you not troubled by the irony? That, in order to fight for freedom, women must not be free? Your deflection away from her as a vital, unique individual and onto the 'class' is a transparent strategy, and I'll let you know it won't fly with me. You've no right to shame and silence her by invoking mythical 'others' she has no responsibility for… especially when I've established that the point is not the *choice*: it's the ability to make that choice, ANY choice, *free from all judgment*. And that's the part you seem stubbornly to be missing. Nobody forced Casey to do it: no-one was holding a gun to her head, nothing was against her will. She *chose* to do it. And I'm reliably informed she had the largest amount of creative input into the shoot, too! As she says in the interview that I read, for *her*, at that moment, doing that photo shoot made her happy. And if that's not what feminism is all about, then I don't know what is! But if people like you choose to objectify her rather than to appreciate the beauty of her choice—well, let's focus on that problem, and get about fixing it. Please. If I may say so, Rachel, and still keep this conversation within the bounds of courtesy (because it may surprise you to learn that courtesy is not just a political strategy or cause: it's just being polite), that argument is nothing more than a load of judgmental, ignorant horseshit. You say they *can* choose to do whatever they want while you're sitting there disapproving of them, but why should they have to put up with your criticism when they do it? The only thing you're establishing here is that it's the job of women to scold *other women* for not being feminist enough … Yes, yes you are. You have the right to criticise another woman's personal choices for self-expression? I mean, have you read Anne Summers? You clearly seem not to have—or you've missed the entire central theme of the text. I think perhaps you need to reflect on your *own* behaviour. You see, it's not even your 'take' on feminism that bothers me, it's your act of exclusion. You have effectively barred Casey from any participation in feminist activism because she doesn't conform to your arbitrary standards. You're also trying to do it to me, *and* accusing me of occluding you, despite me trying to courteously engage with you on this very important topic while you resort to profanity and insults (*gendered* insults, I might add). Frankly, I'm very close to being done with you. This was a conversation *I* started, you inserted yourself into it, and you've been nothing but rude while I've been unfailingly polite and respectful. No, I do support you, Rachel; I support you in making any choices you like for *your* life. Just like I support all women. But you are now trying to make choices for *my* life and you do not get to do that. You have the right to make any comment you like of your own somewhere else; and, then, if *I* want to engage with *you*, I have the right to choose to respond. That's the freedom you have, and that's the freedom I have. But you don't want to do that: you want to police everyone else's discussion and opinions, and I'm simply not going to stand back and let you do that. Please, just be quiet. You are not going to achieve anything further, and any more of these attempts at brow-beating will deny you the dignity of leaving while courtesy is still possible. But I mustn't allow myself to sink down to your level, so I'm going to make one last attempt at bringing this back into the realm of rational debate. See if you can simmer down enough to participate in a civil manner, Rachel. Emma Goldman's writings are quite instructive here, and I think you could learn a lot from them. One particular part leaps to mind … it's here on my phone: 'At the dances I was one of the most untiring and gayest. One evening a cousin of Sasha, a young boy, took me aside. With a grave face, as if he were about to announce the death of a dear comrade, he whispered to me that it did not behove an agitator to dance. Certainly not with such reckless abandon, anyway. My frivolity would only hurt the Cause.' You see, she could not believe, Rachel, that he thought it was his right, his *privilege*, to throw her ideology back in her face like it was a weapon with which to strike her. Feminism, just like anarchism, is not one-size-fits-all—that kind of prescriptivism belongs to fascism and the kind of dictatorial trolls you should really be spending your time on, if you ask me. 'Flagellation by rule' is not the domain of egalitarian ideals that only want to champion individual freedom and choice. And no, no—excuse me, Rachel, but that is *socialism*. Not feminism. And your dogmatic insistence that Casey posing for a risqué photo somehow damages the cause of womankind *clearly* demonstrates that you've missed the point. Goldman finishes with the following condemnation, and I think it is instructive for you. Pay attention, Rachel: 'I did not believe that a Cause which stood for a beautiful ideal, for anarchism, for release and freedom from convention and prejudice, should demand the denial of life and joy. I insisted that our Cause could not expect me to become a nun and that the movement would not be turned into a cloister. If it meant that, I did not want it.' You are failing to allow people to just be themselves, whatever that entails, and you are turning this movement into Goldman's cloister. This is what she has to say about your brand of feminism, Rachel, and this is what I have to say, too. If there is to be no dancing, I want none of your revolution! No, you can't seem to let me have the last word, can you? I have *repeatedly* stated that my idea of liberation means personal freedom for *everyone*, regardless of the level of privilege they may or may not experience. You say I fail to account for disenfranchised women when, *in fact*, my definition includes enfranchising all those women and giving them exactly the same choice that Casey has here. I would have thought that part of it was self-evident. Every woman should be allowed to pursue activities that make her happy, regardless of whether she's poor, coloured, young, old, anything— and that includes choosing whether to pose alluringly for a magazine cover if that's what she has decided is the way she wants to express herself and is what brings her joy. Because that's obviously what I meant by, 'If there is to be no dancing.' I meant, 'If there is to be no joy.' Which I'm pretty sure you understood, and you just chose to misinterpret me instead. *My* world is a world of personal freedom for *all* women—that's what you should be fighting for. And every time you judge and pick on the way women exercise that freedom, according to some subjective assessment of whether *you* think their behaviour advances the cause of womankind or not, we lose the very thing for which we are fighting, Rachel: we lose the joy.

# 16

# Sympathetic White Women Talk Music at Brunch

## *Audrey El-Osta*

I'm the latte, she's the flat white, thanks. But like,
you have to watch Nicki in the 'Monster' video,
because while you can hear her
characters in her verse you have to see
the woman talking to herself, no, *selves*
to really get how the Harajuku
Barbie is imprisoned by that Roman
Zolanski, you know what I mean? Like Barbie
is meant to be this hyper-feminine
Madonna / virgin / innocent perfect
against Roman, clearly represented
as whore, derelict, sexual, queer, mad
woman in the attic! This inner battle,
this cataclysmic collision of male
and female, the Cockney Creole
and the Queens dialectic crash;
        I had the smashed avo, thanks!
Nicki killed that track and proved
that the self is split and blurred along
intersecting identities
acceptance is a battleground between lion, goat, dragon
        Sorry, this was meant to be poached.
and victory will be a bloody mess
treading on eggshells of the being born

in the ashes—You've lost control of this
metaphor, phoenix or chimera?
—You can't choose! It's both, all of the above;
ashes, wreckage, firebomb, split atom
banging big to birth
an absolute, motherfucking, monster!

# big fish little fish

## *Brent Cantwell*

After the dance—*big fish little fish*
*Put it in a box*—we seek crepuscular
Corners—chill-out rooms—to flesh out each foot
With words like *concupiscent   muscular* ...

Men submit to shape  sweat-salt 'n' sinew
In the half-light   on a hot plate sizzling
Everything that feels possible in you
We move slower without thought here out in

The never-places  where lip-stuck faces
Pare treacherous words down to the iamb
A butterfly sits where my heart paces
I answer the pin   *I am who   I am* ...

A poised lepidopterist bops and clocks
*Big fish little fish   put me in a box*

# 18

# At the Window

## *Kim Waters*

The truth is
it's a boring painting,
one of those impressionistic-
follower types that are going to make you
write lines like:
'Seated in the open arrival of the day
a woman pauses for company in the too bright
light of the morning.'
And then you get stuck,
your pencil between your teeth,
drawing out words like 'drinkable,'
'vessel' and 'brimmed.'
You try to be clever and
make something of the clock
ticking beyond the frame,
but like the glassware
on that foreign woman's table
it's pretty transparent and
the painting's not worth
the poem it belongs to.

# 19

# The Lady Who Walks

## *Ann Jackson*

JOINT WINNER OF THE MONASH
UNDERGRADUATE PRIZE FOR
CREATIVE WRITING

I was never particularly nice to my mother. I guess I found it hard to forgive her for being Chinese. We lived together with my dad, who never saw a foreign shore in his life, in a flat that was really only meant for two people.

I'm not sure exactly when the walking started. It was just something that happened naturally, like fruit coming into season. Ma would be up at six thirty and out the door in ten minutes. I knew because the walls were so thin you could always tell what everyone else was up to. After I heard the front door click shut, sometimes I would push the curtain aside and watch as she set off down the street.

These days when I think about Ma, the funny thing is that I can't picture her face properly. But I can see her tiny figure as she marches down the footpath, pumping her arms back and forth with a fierce determination.

\*\*\*

One morning—I reckon I must've been eight or so—a boy came and spoke to me at recess. 'That lady who walks all the time, she's your mum, right?' When I didn't reply he went on: 'My uncle saw her this morning.'

I said: 'Is he okay? He'd better wash his eyes out quick!'

That was the first time I'd ever gotten a laugh out of my classmates. It gave me a warm shiver in my belly.

That very same day, a girl I'd never spoken to sat next to me at lunch. She had a brown ponytail and freckles on her nose. She told me I was lucky, being able to eat Chinese food whenever I wanted. I wasn't sure how to reply to that so I offered her some of my chicken rice instead and we ended up trading lunches.

When I got home I told Dad I'd made a new friend. I pretended it was no big deal but he could tell how pleased I was. Ma was busy in the kitchen and I didn't think she'd even heard. But at dinnertime when she clunked the bowl down in front of me, there was an extra fried egg sitting on top of my noodles.

***

I was ten when I first joined Ma for one of her walks. I remember because that year she'd insisted on a big birthday celebration, as if reaching double digits was some kind of momentous occasion. This particular morning Dad urged me to tag along with her. 'Go on. She'd be stoked,' he said. It wasn't exactly my idea of a morning pick-me-up. But for once I didn't whinge, just slipped on a pair of thongs and followed Ma out the door, slapping away flies.

It was the middle of summer and even at this hour, the air was warm and sluggish. My shirt was sticky with sweat and I knew my ears were bright red.

This was the first time I'd walked Ma's route: past the IGA, through the park, around the school and back again. I must've been afraid someone would see us together as we passed the school, because I began talking to Ma in a short, stiff manner so as to not appear too close. She didn't seem to notice.

We'd just reached the park when Ma grabbed my arm with a gasp. 'Lu, look!'

I looked. A fly was tickling the back of my neck and Ma's fingers were pressing into my arm. She was pointing to a cluster of small red apples, smiling like she'd stumbled across some buried treasure. Before I could say anything, she began to rip the fruit off the branch and stash them in the green recyclable bag she was carrying.

The fly buzzed in my ear, making me jump violently. 'Ma,' I hissed, glancing up and down the street to make sure no-one was around. 'Are you sure that's allowed?'

Ma shrugged and reached for another apple. 'But no-one has taken them. They'll be wasted.'

Maybe it was the heat—I've never had much of a tolerance for hot weather—but, all of a sudden, I felt hugely irritated with Ma.

'Stop it!'

I pushed the bag out of her hand.

Apples rolled across the dirt. Ma squinted at me for a moment, as if I were an odd word she couldn't quite figure out. Then she shook her head and made a clucking noise—like I was the one who was loopy—and squatted to gather the fallen apples.

I hesitated. I think I'd expected her to snap back at me or something. But now there was no easy way to make things right. I muttered something about heading home. The words dangled stupidly in the air, and after a few seconds I marched off.

When I reached the edge of the park I looked back. Ma was down on all fours, snatching up the dusty apples and shovelling them into that old green bag as if her life depended on it.

\*\*\*

One morning I woke up and there was no porridge waiting. Dad made Vegemite on toast. It tasted dry and stuck in my throat. Dad said he'd wait a couple more minutes then take the car out to look for Ma. He told me not to worry.

When the phone rang he leapt up like he'd been shot. Only once we were heading down the road did Dad tell me that Ma had tried to enter someone else's flat. 'Maybe it looked sort of like ours,' I said, and mumbled something about having seen plenty of dingy white buildings around. It was the first time I'd heard of Ma being, you know, not quite right up there. So I wasn't exactly sure what to say.

When we got to the police station Ma was smaller than I remembered, like she'd shrunk into herself. There was a trickle of dried blood from her nostril. The cop was chewing gum. He said Ma had become violent when he'd tried to get her to leave the block of flats. It seemed unbelievable. Dad was the one who smacked me when I was mucking about. I'd never even seen Ma hit a fly with a rolled-up newspaper.

*\*\**

Dad said one of us had to accompany Ma every time she left the house. On Saturdays, that unlucky person was me. I set my alarm to six. If Ma went off by herself, Dad would yell at me later. It was like the more patience he spent on her, the less was left for me.

When Ma saw me coming her face lit up with a smile. She kept patting my arm with her small hand as we trudged down the footpath. 'Lu,' she'd say, 'look at that lovely big fruit. Like *youzi*. You know *youzi*? Can feed a whole family.'

I spoke as little as possible. I guess I was still a bit scared that somebody might see us together. At first Ma didn't seem to mind, but slowly, our conversations shrivelled and died. She still liked to point things out—maybe an early plum blossom, or a blackbird startled into flight—but it was as if she'd lost the words to say how beautiful they were. And for me, it seemed like far too much effort to do anything other than nod and keep walking.

Dad was awfully patient with Ma, always ready with a smile and the old dictionary so she could point to the words she couldn't pronounce. Somehow he managed to figure out exactly what she wanted each time; I never bothered.

It took me several months to realise she'd stopped talking altogether. I'm not proud of it. I assumed Ma had simply accepted that I wasn't interested in making conversation. It was only when she began to speak Chinese that I realised just how much her English had been chewed away.

I suppose I should make it clear that Ma had never spoken to me in Chinese before. Dad said it was because she'd wanted me to speak English like a native. Of course, I'd heard the rapid-fire string of swear words that spilled out when she broke a plate or burned herself on the kettle, so I wasn't completely ignorant of the language. But the first time she turned to me and spoke in Chinese, the best reply I could give her was a blank stare.

Dad bought me a couple of textbooks but I never found the time to get very far. Weeks bled into months. Ma would step outside with dried porridge crusted on her upper lip and her shoelaces undone. When I bent down to help her, I could smell her stale sweat—she'd forgotten to wash again.

She would often reach a corner and head down the wrong street without the slightest hesitation. On the particular morning I'm thinking of, we'd just circled the primary school when she paused at the edge of the park. When I pointed her in the right direction she nodded and said something to me in Chinese.

It took a few moments to register. I knew very little of the language, but the words were straight off the first page of the textbook. The translation: 'Thank you, miss.' And underneath, in fine black print: *Used to address a stranger.*

\*\*\*

The year I turned thirteen, Ma stopped walking.

She slept a lot and when she woke she was always irritable, so I preferred it when she was asleep. If there were roadworks in the street or the neighbours were having a party we would suddenly hear this bellowing, and Dad would jump out of his seat and run to Ma's room. Only he could calm her down. Afterwards he'd apologise to the neighbours, as if what Ma did were his fault.

We never talked much about our feelings, but I could tell Dad was pretty cut up about everything that happened to Ma. After she passed he kind of let himself go. It was like he'd been holding together all these years for her sake. Dad's sister Julie moved in to give us a hand. She had a prickly temper, but she could tell when I needed space and knew how to cook a fine roast lamb.

By then I was in high school so it was a while before I went back to the park and saw that the apple tree—you know, the one Ma'd been nicking fruit from—wasn't there anymore. Maybe it'd been pulled out or maybe it just died, I don't know. But it was a bit of a shock. It kind of made me realise that Ma was gone. Like, really gone.

\*\*\*

Sometimes I jolt awake at six. It's actually a bit creepy. Not that I believe Ma's spirit is hanging about or anything like that. Still, I pull on a pair of jeans and a t-shirt and head off into the cold crisp morning.

I take Ma's route just out of habit. The IGA's bigger now. There's a bunch of new shops, with some of the stuff you could only buy at the city market before. They've even got sticky rice cakes out for the New Year. I picked up a packet the other day, thinking I'd share them with Julie and Dad. I'd just stashed them in one of my bags along with the dried noodles and the rest of the groceries when I heard a woman say: 'Look, isn't that her? You know, the lady who walks in the mornings.' My bags fell with a thump; one of them burst open and apples tumbled across the floor. I scanned the aisles desperately for the shrunken form of my mother. Finally I caught sight of the woman who'd spoken and realised she'd been pointing at me.

My ears burned with embarrassment but I managed a smile. She came over to help me gather the bruised apples. Together we knelt on the floor and packed them into my bag—gently, as if each one was a treasure.

*First published in* Voiceworks *#103 'Bang' (2016).*

20

# Belated Bulletin

## *Allan Lake*

*(for Myuran Sukumaran & Andrew Chan)*

Why I walked along this canal
while you approached death from
a different direction is a mixture
of fate and luck for which there
seems no guide. In youth I too
provoked gods and law enforcers,
could have ended elsewhere
if shiny things had beckoned.
From a platform I might have
leapt upon the tracks to fetch
a golden ring but no ring fell
so I am calm by this canal
while your hearts are shattered.

Slight breeze rattles leaves on
this spring day. Blue of sky
accentuated by almost pure
white cumulus that look solid,
trees, grass and canal moss
backdropping contentment,
an idyllic construct somewhere
between Bali heat and Antarctica.
Sudden shots

from a nail gun do not startle
the black swans or their hapless
cygnets on the murky water,
which makes its way to cleansing sea.
Happened before; it'll happen again
as long as people want things.

* *Sukumaran & Chan: Two Australian drug traffickers executed by firing squad in Bali.*

# 21

# William Drummond's Resting Place

## *Jena Woodhouse*

Drummond's tomb was empty as the woods in winter, all forlorn.
Drifts of dead leaves lay knee-deep in gloom beneath the lichened roof,
Along with juice cartons and cans, offerings of graveyard trash.

Freshets from a spring still rise from somewhere in that cemetery
And flow beneath the turf and tree roots to a well, the Eldin spout,
Whose waters, once revered as the elixir of longevity,
Stagnate inside The Laird and Dog, undrinkable and sad.

If Drummond leads a spectral life, look elsewhere for his legacy.
Seeking comfort, seeking light, he hastens back to Hawthornden,
In whose warm rooms late at night guest writers dream or lie awake,
Listening to owls and the incessant purling of the Esk, which hasn't
Altered course since Drummond walked beside it, solitary—
In mourning for Miss Cunninghame—or in the company of friends.

Ethereal, he lingers at closed portals, envious of sleep,
Listening for sounds of pages turning, signs of wakefulness.
Once, the presence at my door was so intense, I turned the key,
As if a lock were likely to deter a homing revenant.

Morning shepherded me back to oatmeal porridge, urgent drafts—
Volatile ideas that vied for egress, jockeying for space
As horses champ and chafe against the chute, impatient for the start.

Yet as guests pace the narrow path beneath the crags of roseate stone,
Turning images this way and that in the alembic light,
Who can be sure he isn't there, watching from his mossy throne,
Hewn from a rock that marks his place and mocks the vacant tomb.

*William Drummond of Hawthornden (1585–1649)—Scottish poet and man of letters, friend of Ben Jonson (1572–1637), second laird of Hawthornden, now Hawthornden Castle International Writers' Retreat.*

# 22

# Glass

## *Lauren Burridge*

HIGHEST-PLACING MONASH UNIVERSITY
STUDENT IN THE MONASH UNDERGRADUATE
PRIZE FOR CREATIVE WRITING

I know that man. Know his family, too. Always thought his sister would go first—she's had skin cancer twice—but no, Cherry is being lowered into the grave after only twenty-six years out of the womb. His mother, Debbie, never saw her angel boy with his shirt off. Couldn't see anything in the way he waved his hands when he spoke. Precious, only leaving her bereft of grandchildren and a stale room to clear out. She'll cling to that memory so tight that it's swollen beyond recognition, while his father turns to the book, turns to drink. I have a taste for whiskey myself.

Our little group has good intentions. Give him our prayers, send him off. Bleach his history so the older guests don't storm out of the cemetery. Reassure his mother. Comfort her, yes, he's in a better place. Remind his sister to keep her hat on, and did you put sunscreen on before going outside?

None of them know him like I do. Even his dad, who found him sprawled on the pavement, cherry-blood staining his skin, doesn't know him like I always have.

He had a knack for getting on people's nerves. It was the child in him, or the rebel, whose honesty sparked riots in every bar we went to. A bad sort of honesty, where his eyebrows arched up and pinned themselves to his hairline whenever he spoke. Something he took up from necessity.

'Crush, or be crushed,' he says through the lacquered wood. 'A defence made of swords that others have thrust.'

I knew before he knew the words. A month later he dyed his hair pink on a whim and had two hours to change it back before his parents came home. He was at my door, his fingers the colour of wet candy floss.

'Shaney, gimme your goddamn car keys. Need to get to the shops ay-sap.'

'Fairy hair ain't so bad, is it?'

'If it's on your son, yeah, it is.' We dyed it back on time. No harm done, except for a telltale towel we burnt as his parents rolled up into the driveway.

I wonder if they removed his piercings when they lie him in his casket. A left lobe to match mine, a knot through his tongue. Another ring only I'd seen.

'Let them have it,' he'd say. 'I'm a ghost-stuffed meat-bag anyway.' The way he saw it, the moment your fluids froze, the body and spirit separated, plunging the latter into, and I quote the witty fucker, 'everlasting delirium'. Neither of us thought he'd get to try it so soon.

***

It's time for his mother to give a eulogy. Clawing against gravity and grief, she pulls out a quaking piece of paper from her handbag. She talks about the day he was born. How he entered the world in stagnant water, saved by the miraculous grace of a surgeon. She touches the scar he left across her belly. She recalls his first cries.

She starts off his childhood around the time I met him. She sent him off one afternoon, sweltering, to the pool with his sister. The two come back smelling of chlorine, their hair cow-licked. Popsicles rolling onto their hands, leaving long lines like snail slime. Sticky like snail slime too. Turns out the pair forgot to bring sunscreen and spent all afternoon under the glare. Sonja, preteen by then, flaunts her tan. But Cherry, the poor kid, doesn't have the skin for it, and from his forehead to the collar of his rashie his flesh is pricked pink. Debbie, looking at his cheeks swollen with popsicle, can't contain herself. Laughs her hat off. Catches Cherry's resemblance to a certain two-bulbed fruit and loses it again. The nickname sticks all through primary school, until everyone forgets it but me.

That story is the only good part of her spiel, in my opinion.

Oh, she peddles her way through his life. Then she errs on the most important part. She skips his second birth. A rebirth, no cord to sever.

His mother, bless her, didn't know. Or refused to know. Deluded herself until her boy was still her boy.

Born again at sixteen. My house, vodka on our lips nicked from my mum's bedside table. She's at work. Cherry lying half-stripped on the sofa, sweat crawling across his belly. I trace circles over and over on his chest.

Three boys come to the window looking for a fight. We meet them outside. One says I hit on him. Fondled him with my eyes. He starts name calling. Things not worth repeating, really. But they work well enough to make Cherry pop his top.

Afterwards, I bend sorely to the pavement, pick up a tooth and shoot it at them through my fingers.

Cherry copped a lot. Too much to hide from his wailing mum. My boy, my brave boy—I'll go to the school, give those bullies what they deserve—sweet boy. His dad huffed in approval, but I saw his sideways glances. Likely had his suspicions then. Lucky for Cherry, the old man couldn't pick out the hickeys from the bruises.

We went out again that night. Patched up, wrapped up. Too hot for shirts, even past dusk. We left them hanging on my letterbox.

He told me there was no going back. It was us, in every meaning of the phrase, against them. Black and white. Zebra stripes. At some point he threw his arms around my shoulders. Puckered up, smacked my dry lips with his, then spun and ran the other way. Skipped, shimmied down the road. Flaunted his middle fingers for the neighbours.

'Come get me, fuckers, I'm right here. I am. I am.'

That was the thickest day of our lives. In three acts: finding, fighting, flaunting. Nothing made him feel more alive.

Debbie finishes. Her husband moves to cradle her and draw her back into the crowd. A few more words sweep across the grave and it's over.

Sonja, Cherry's sister, rushes over to catch my sleeve. I can't look at her. She's got his eyes.

'You're coming to the reception,' she says.

'Of course. Wouldn't miss it.'

'Do you have a ride?' She's still holding me. Those fingers pinching my suit jacket lock me down like crocodile jaws.

'I borrowed a friend's car.'

'I'll see you there, then.'

Satisfied, she releases me. She turns and goes to her parents. The shoulder of her shawl slips, freckled skin exposed. Debbie pulls it up like she's naked.

Asks her again about sunscreen. It's so obvious; the old woman cares more than she does.

The congregation does well to hold itself together within the yellow walls of Debbie's home. Her best lace runner lies prostrate on the kitchen table. A collection of flowers line the mantelpiece. Respectful chatter ebbs neck-deep.

Cherry's dad looks as eager to speak to me as I to him. He stays put in the swamp of work friends drinking in the hallway. Debbie has long since left the house. She spoke to Sonja some time ago before slipping out the back door through the laundry. Probably shuffling alongside the creek a block down the road, feeling stagnant with the smell of it.

Sonja splits her time between the hors d'oeuvres and extended family. I feel her eyes on my collar as she passes through the lounge to the kitchen, kitchen to the hall.

One of the uncles in the room—a silver fox—slides on over to the fireplace for a chat. He comments on the wallpaper while adjusting his tie.

'Atrocious. What's yer name?'

'Shane.' Handshake. 'Are you—'

'An uncle, yep. Kid had a few. You a workmate of his, Shane?'

'Housemate, actually.'

'Ah.' Does a slight bow with his eyes. He's thinking: 'Have fun with the cleanup.'

'So, whaddaya do?' he asks.

'I'm a teacher.'

'Whaddaya teach?'

'High school P.E.'

'Good on you. Shaping young bodies.'

Sonja wafts past, tray heavy with glasses. The uncle catches a glimpse and excuses himself, slinking off toward the drinks.

A morning comes to mind while I stand there, waiting for the reception to be over. I couldn't describe the weather if I wanted to; Cherry and I hadn't moved since waking. Both of us stuffed into a single bed in case his parents came to visit. A weekend gone by since we moved in, and all we'd unpacked were the curtains. Our belongings still piled high like cardboard skyscrapers through the house.

I'm halfway back to snoring when he gets an idea. I see it twitching behind his eyes. He springs up off the mattress and starts clawing his way through our cardboard city.

'Close yer eyes.'

Beneath the doona I hear him shuffling about. Two sharp sounds, solid points striking the floor. The clumsy steps of a newborn deer.

'Alright, have a look.'

His head comes into view first: hair tousled the way I left it, goofy grin widening. Nude shoulders, arms folded across his chest, pinning a sheet to his body like a makeshift robe. Then a leg, protruding from the fabric, long and bony, bends into a pointed high-heeled shoe. The colour of mustard, for God's sake.

Surprise renders it even funnier. I can barely breathe—he looks fantastic.

'Where in hell did you get those?'

He pinches his lips tight, raises his eyebrows—the eyebrows, for Chrissake—brushes the question away, and begins to strut. Feet placed like on a tightrope, he weaves between the box towers, betraying grace with an occasional loss of balance. Follows his heels on a beeline to the door. I pause between cackles to wolf-whistle.

\*\*\*

There's an image of him pasted to the inside of my skull. For the next week it's all I think about. I see a coffin underwater. Just like the one he's in now, only the top is made of glass. Cherry's skin is glass too. With his arms by his sides, the whole front of him is see-through. Beneath his ribs his cold heart throbs. More than anything it makes me want to cry.

\*\*\*

'I didn't catch you after the funeral.'

Sonja. At the door. Her car boot ajar. There's cardboard boxes piled along the hallway. Each one is labelled 'memories.'

'I was there. Didn't leave early.'

'It was super busy. Could you give me a hand?'

I pick up 'music.' Plastic casings slide within. They strike the walls with their corners, try punching their way out of the cardboard. She slips past me into the house and takes a box of Cherry's stuff. Debbie wants to sort it herself. I'm here to help the courier.

She's taking everything but a T-shirt I've hidden and a canvas print of a Banksy. Cherry said once that it was like a telescope pointed at his soul.

It hurts, but I ask her.

'Do you think you'll keep much of this stuff?'

She pauses, as if involuntarily. Returns quickly back to hauling boxes.

'I don't know. Mum has a shed out the back, so . . .'

We both know it's full of car parts. She could at least try to fool me.

We finish loading Cherry's stuff into the boot. I wait for Sonja to leave. She takes a breather, leans back on her car, her elbows protruding like chicken wings. We look over to the house. Through the open front door, the hall lies empty like a flushed artery. We stay for a moment, lamenting our loss. Then she says something that damn near breaks my heart all over again.

'I bought him those mustard heels.'

I can't think of anything but Cherry: eyebrows arched, wrists bent over the sheet with faux delicacy. Looking better in those shoes than anyone else ever could.

My absence must show on my face. Sonja steps into my view, taking up everything.

'I consider you family, Shane. Always have. I want to thank you for loving Samuel like he deserved.'

Then her hair is in my mouth and in my eyes. She holds me like that for a while.

She moves back, pulls her hair into place. There's a shiny scar on the side of her nose. It's embedded into her skin like a snowflake on sand. She is golden and freckled, with neat teeth. Her laugh lines fold neatly into a compact early-thirties face.

She holds her gaze steady on me, a pale grey pair so familiar I could sink into them.

'Call me if you need anything,' she says, leaving.

Our life wrapped into a neat little package. She unravels it, pulls it open by the strings. Sits back and regards its beauty.

The image of the coffin is back. Cherry's transparent chest. I've been found by the only other person who saw through his glass skin. He's here, in her, in me. He's running down our street at sixteen, buck-naked, shouting.

Here I am. I am. I am.

23

# The £1000 Bend

*T Venessa Nguyen*

The £1000 Bend
is scraping thin
between two things
that will not ever meet.
It's holding onto handrails just out of reach;
the brightly painted bars
running overhead but not ahead
to hold you steady
as the faint electric whistle
cultivates a home
against the rhythm of your dreams.

Sometimes it lives in scared strewn things
screaming Shakespeare in reverse
too afraid to sit amongst the people
gambling on their £1000 bends.
It breaks the bones
of suburban homes
struggling to find a foothold in a crowd
as the tunnel closes in
at six o'clock
and the rails are beaten to a bend.

It's warping iron tracks
and making glitter from graffiti,
pretending to be Michelangelo

praying in ¾ time
along a soundscape uninvented
and unparalleled.
You break facades
and paint them fresh,
tattoo the underground with compositions
and listen to the echoes
that beat like broken metronomes
skipping inside bars untimed
to the direction leading home.

You breathe the £1000 bend
like it's the thing with feathers
and dare to waltz into skies of grey
as the weather stains in untimed droplets
to cries of engines and of people
who all start to look and feel the same.

Route maps and itineraries line your pockets
wearing along well folded lines,
as they leave unappreciated
little scabs of second-hand existence
in a notebook of apologies.

But before the steamrolled tracks
grind to a stop
you cannot drop
your fearless gaze.
Having lived, and breathed, and gambled,
and lost
you continue to bend
a thousand pounds to search your soul.

# 24

# Torn Identity

## *Ashvini Ahilan*

It was the University of Surrey's regular student party night known as 'Citrus.' Hockey players, netballers, footballers, and anyone keen for a boozy night and hook-up mingled together for the biggest 'party night' of the week. The music pulsed around me as I stood at the bar, waiting to be served. My eyes roved around the crowded club and spotted smug, drunk rugby players in their shirts and ties, hair combed back, flirting with girls. Some of the girls looked star-struck, some of them even fawned over these privileged, preppy athletes who were like celebrities on campus. I turned away in disgust. Don't get me wrong, while I can certainly appreciate a well-built, athletic guy, I was annoyed at the sight of these entitled boys being worshipped.

Not too long after, I noticed that one of these boys had sidled up to me. He straightened his tie and attempted to strike up a conversation. I smiled politely and listened to him complain about the slow bar service. And then he asked the question.

'So where are you from?'

Because I was less interested in him, and more interested in getting my drink and returning to the dance floor, I replied 'I'm staying at Battersea Court.'

He laughed, 'No, where are you *from*?' he questioned again.

'I'm from London,' I smiled, 'East London, really.'

He shook his head, smiling, 'No, what I mean is, where are your parents from?'

'Ooooh, they are from Sri Lanka.' I said, finally addressing his real question. He was asking about my heritage and ethnicity. Having been born and raised in London, I had always identified myself as British. But in his eyes, I was an Other, I was from elsewhere.

For this boy, and many others, the colour of my skin dictates my identity. In his ground-breaking book, *Black Skin, White Masks*, Frantz Fanon observes that, 'colour is the most obvious manifestation of race [and] has been the criterion by which men are judged.'[1] My 'true identity' was usually based on the colour of my skin and where my 'parents were from.' Where I was born and lived all of my life seemed to carry little weight in brief social interactions like this one. At the time, it was only a minor annoyance. But it wasn't until I began studying Post-Colonial theory in my second year of university that I began to understand how routine such encounters could be.

University studies opened my eyes to the legacy of Colonialism. I was introduced to writing by Salman Rushdie, Homi Bhabha and Edward Said, that shaped the way I see the world and myself in it as a second-generation immigrant. I was taken by Monica Ali's *Brick Lane* and Kureshi's *The Buddha of Suburbia*; stories that focus on the lives and unique struggles of second-generation immigrants. These stories suggested new ways to negotiate one's identity. Karim, the main character in *Buddha of Suburbia*, rejects the Colonial concept of identity as being a binary. This is particularly evident in the opening lines of the novel in which he repeatedly states how he is an Englishman. He instead sees himself as being a 'new breed...emerging from two histories.'[2] Karim rejects the Western ideology of identity as being fixed. Stories such as this resonated with me: all my life I had felt the tension between my identity as a British citizen and my status as a child of refugees who were forced to flee their country in a bid to save their lives.

The whole island of Sri Lanka, formerly known as Ceylon, was under British administration in 1833. Despite many complications, it eventually gained independence in 1948. Colonial rule, however, had already created social unrest. Thus, soon after, a divide between Sri Lankan Tamils and Sinhalese people quickly developed, leading to the start of the Sri Lankan Civil War in 1983.[3] According to a government statement, a UN panel 'estimated that around 40,000 died [during the course of the war], while other independent reports estimated the number of civilians dead to exceed

1   Frantz Fanon, *Black Skin, White Masks*. Pluto Press, 1986, p. 118.
2   Hanif Kureishi, *Buddha of Suburbia*. Penguin Books USA Inc., 1990, p. 3.
3   'Sri Lanka Country Profile.' *BBC World News*, BBC News, 18 Apr. 2017. http://www.bbc.com/news/world-south-asia-11999611.

100,000.[4] Some even argued that the events amounted to ethnic cleansing by the Sri Lankan government. Because of such political violence, my parents felt forced to leave their country: their homeland had become a war zone.

In 1983, riots had broken out in the city of Colombo. Tamil homes were looted and set on fire. Months after the sudden death of my grandfather and the subsequent looting of their family home by rioters, my mother and her family had taken shelter with a neighbour, hoping the unrest would eventually settle down. When tensions did not seem to be diminishing quickly enough, they decided to move to Canada. My aunt, who was the eldest daughter of the family, had already left for Canada months before. The rest of the family followed close behind.

My father had not faced personal attacks himself. But he once described bearing witness to the suffering of others—neighbours, family members, children. He described it as 'indirect, unbearable mental agony.' Ten members of my father's huge family moved one-by-one to England in 1984 and three were separated to Canada. However, in doing so, their family was temporarily disrupted due to immigration issues—a situation all too common for many refugees and asylum seekers. Their family was torn apart in attempts to gain some stability and ultimately safety.

Moving to new countries proved to be a difficult adjustment for both of my parents. They were both made to find and work menial jobs in order to ensure that they played their part in helping their families stand on their own two feet. Amongst financial struggles, they had to learn to navigate the new cultural contexts they found themselves within. My dad had to adjust to a 'Westernised' life at university, whilst also working part-time to support his family. My mother, on the other hand, had to navigate through her teenage years at a high school in Montreal, a high school, which required that she become fluent not only in English but also French. Throughout their lives, they faced repeated acts of racism and were often ridiculed for their appearance and accent. Racism was an added weight to the financial and emotional burdens they faced. But, eventually, they learnt to accept it as a part of their daily lives: it became a new normal and it extended to their work lives.

---

4    Krista Mahr. 'Sri Lanka to start a Tally of Civil-War Dead.' *World Time*, Time, Nov. 28 2013, http://world.time.com/2013/11/28/sri-lanka-to-start-tally-of-civil-war-dead.

When I was young, my mother worked as an assistant teacher and she faced regular torment from children, who would often make gibes at her on account of her accent. Her authority in class was sometimes completely undermined by a factor which was irrelevant to her performing her job well. My dad faced racial discrimination in the workplace from his boss which, coupled with a major car accident and threat of being made redundant, led to him resigning from his job. It was no wonder that he suffered from depression and lay on our sofa for days on end. Since I was only a child, I couldn't completely understand the extent to which racism was collectively taking a toll on our family.

In spite of their many hardships, my parents continued to fight for a stable home. Dad eventually found a way out of the dark murkiness that threatened to engulf him, and he opened his own business. He was able to make a living to financially support our family. Meanwhile, my mum worked hard, studied part-time, took care of our family and got qualifications to work as a counsellor. They both continue to work hard to ensure that my sister and I have a comfortable life.

As a child of immigrants, I have faced racial discrimination on many occasions. Sometimes it was subtle, other times blatant. Although these experiences were not always comparable to those endured by my parents, the life of a second-generation immigrant comes with its own set of problems. My experiences of racial discrimination were sometimes subtle. As a child I was often mimicked by white British children for having a South Asian accent, although I was born in England and many of my friends here in Australia hear a strong British accent. At other times, my dark skin colour was the subject of racist commentary. My supposed accent and outward appearance seemed to be a source of humour to wider society. Not one to passively accept abuse, I would often resist and speak out against such slurs, although there were times when I felt like I couldn't or didn't want to.

As I grew older I became deeply aware of the stigma attached to my culture, its practices, and traditions. Those of us who enjoyed dressing up in Tamil clothes, listening to Tamil music, or eating Tamil food were often pejoratively labelled 'freshies' (as in 'fresh off the boat'). To avoid this stigma and mockery, I began to draw away from my Tamil culture. Indeed, I started to view my culture with embarrassment. Instead, I attempted to fit in with children at my school and shied away from discussing my heritage and culture out of fear of being called a 'freshie.' This sometimes included small gestures that erased the difference signified by my skin: I introduced myself as 'Ash' rather than Ashvini so that people could properly pronounce my name and I avoided joining any cliques that wholly consisted of Tamil people.

My assimilating strategies worked so well that I was regarded (and sometimes self-identified) as a 'coconut'—a derogatory term often used to describe a brown person who supposedly 'acts white.' I internalised the racism that I witnessed and began to ridicule others, calling them 'freshie' and making jokes at their expense. I was conditioned to shame my own culture. Kids who did or said things that strayed from a dominant Colonial ideology of what it meant to be British were picked out and punished. In the school playground, in the classroom, in extra-curricular activities, I was being assimilated into a dominant British culture, adopting the attitudes and habits of the dominant members in society. And so, I lost touch with my Tamil heritage. I was and still am faced with the problem of trying to find my identity, torn between a British identity and the Tamil identity of my ancestors.

At university, I was confronted by a group of South Asian guys who had somehow heard of me from an old school friend. As I introduced myself, they sniggered and replied 'Ohhh you're THE coconut.' Stunned with such a bold accusation, I was rendered speechless and merely stared back. Having not joined the Tamil community at university, I was made to feel ashamed for not having integrated with them. Although, I had not made a conscious effort to assimilate with the Tamil community, I had also not gone out of my way to shun them. This event, among many others, proved my detachment from both the Tamil and Western community. I was stuck, torn, not belonging anywhere.

Although I can understand a good deal of Tamil, I fail to properly speak it. My attempts are often met with mockery from older family members who are amused by my inability to string together a single sentence; and any sentence that I am able to muster always seems to be inflected by my British. Though I'm told I shouldn't let any of this deter me, it's difficult to move past the embarrassment I feel when I try and fail to improve my Tamil speaking. The laughter at my expense doesn't help. Sometimes, I am even scolded by family for having failed to retain my culture and speak my 'mother tongue.' It's not that I am not interested in speaking my mother tongue. Rather, I am faced with the predicament of not properly being able to honour a language that is almost over two thousand years old. I fear not being able to preserve my tradition and culture and to have the ability to pass this on to my own children.

Going to university, I began to see a certain fascination that surrounded my ethnicity. My white friends would often ask me questions about my language, culture and wedding traditions. They often expressed their interest to wear traditional Tamil outfits, saying that they love how a bindi looks. I began to more actively embrace my culture; I felt privileged to have so many new friends show an interest in me, my family and our culture. However, such questions made some of my cultural practices seem exotic and almost foreign. To this day, I am torn between feeling happy that my friends take an interest in my life and being dismayed by their ignorance when they exotify my culture according to the stereotypes of dominant British society.

Not being able to identify exclusively with either Tamil or British culture, I am pulled between two identities: I often feel like I have to choose one over the other. I'm stuck in a state of uncertainty. Though I'm still unsure of my place in society I am more socially aware of the issues that second-generation immigrants have to navigate in order to gain acceptance. Hybridity of identity is brought about by migration and is a product of diaspora. Hybridity is important because it problematises dominant Western attitudes. It complicates the view that there is one way of being 'British' or Australian or American, or any nationality.

These days I embrace this uncertainty within myself, this hybridity. It is a confrontation of Colonial ideology and the racism that comes along with it. Identity cannot be dichotomised and I refuse to be categorised. I am proud of my parents' journeys as immigrants and what they have accomplished despite the immense challenges they've faced. I am unapologetic about who I am. I am proud to be a 'new breed' emerging from two histories.

# Bibliography

Fanon, Frantz. *Black Skin, White Masks*. Pluto Press, 1986.

Kureishi, Hanif. *Buddha of Suburbia*. Penguin Books USA Inc., 1990.

Mahr, Krista. 'Sri Lanka to start a Tally of Civil-War Dead.' *World Time*, Time, Nov. 28 2013, http://world.time.com/2013/11/28/sri-lanka-to-start-tally-of-civil-war-dead

'Sri Lanka Country Profile.' *BBC World News*, BBC News, 18 Apr. 2017, http://www.bbc.com/news/world-south-asia-11999611

# 25

# Lori's Holiday

## *Sivashneel Sanjappa*

Lori was turning thirty in a month and she needed a break. The coming year would be worse than this one.

She must have looked up flights to Fiji about a thousand times in the last two years. At last, she had saved enough money to book the flight and have enough left to enjoy her six days there. She *was* going, nothing would stop her.

It had been a quiet day at the hair salon where she dressed rich ladies' hair, so she had finished work early. The sun was out, the sky was blue, the traffic was light. She threw her bag on the sofa when she got home and opened the windows. The kitchen in her small, one bedroom house smelled of rotting banana peel. She took the bins out. All the while, she hummed an old Island song her grandmother had taught her. After pouring herself a glass of iced tea, she nestled down on the sofa with her laptop.

Once again, she compared the flights across all major airlines. She picked the cheapest one.

Her best friend Sam had already transferred her the money for her own ticket. She, too, had been saving up for months. Her waitress job didn't pay all that much.

Lori had almost clicked 'pay now' when her phone rang.

It was Janine, her sister.

*Oh no, oh God no.*

'Hello?' Lori answered.

'Lori hey, oh how you darling?' Janine asked.

'Are you drunk?'

'No …'

'Oh my god.'

Janine giggled, and hiccupped.

'What do you need?' Lori asked.

'Can you, uhh, can you pick up Mickey from, uh, from school, please Lori?'

'Oh,' Lori let her breath out, 'uh, yes.'

'Thanks sis.'

'For god's sake Jan, it's 2pm on a Thursday.'

Janine was gone.

Lori put her phone down and quickly processed the payment.

A month later, Lori was parked outside her nephew's public school once again. She closed her eyes and tapped the steering wheel, humming her grandma's song.

The school gates opened. Kids spilled out like a broken dam. She spotted her beloved nephew, Mickey, and waved to him.

Mickey got into the car with the familiarity of a joey climbing into its mother's pouch. Without speaking, they decided that a McDonald's run was the right thing for the afternoon.

'Where's Mum?' He asked.

'She's sick, lovely. She'll come get you later.'

'Ok.' Mickey looked away at the other kids playing on the slide.

Mickey fell asleep on the floor of her living room that night, the X-Box controller clenched in his little fists. She tucked him in on her sofa.

Her wild afro sprang back into its usual position when she took the hair-tie off. She pulled out some buds from the top drawer and chucked them into the coffee grinder. Best way to do it. The smell of good weed filled the kitchen. Sam's boyfriend grew them, and she loved Sam even more for it.

She opened her itinerary again and read through the details. Her fingers clutched the phone tightly, as though the itinerary might run away.

It rained the next morning. Lori knelt in front of Mickey, so that her head was sheltered under his umbrella.

'I'm going away in a couple of days honey,' she said to him.

'Why?' he asked.

'For a little holiday.'

'Where?'

'Fiji.'

'Where's that?'

'Not too far from here.'

'You'll come back?'

'I'll be back in no time, because I'll miss you too much.'

She gave her Mickey a squeeze and sent him off. He didn't ask who was picking him up after school.

It would be no use knocking. She unlocked the front door with her spare key and went right into Janine's one bedroom flat. A pair of track pants was strewn on the floor. Thick grey curtains held the daylight at bay.

Even the sound of her barging in didn't wake her sister up. The smell of stale wine seeped out of Janine's bedroom. Along the windows, the thick curtains battled with daylight and banished it to a distant land.

Lori flicked the light switch on.

Janine snored under the quilt. An empty wine glass rose and fell with her breaths. Her wispy hair spilled out from under the covers.

Lori flung the quilt off her sister. It revealed skinny legs and a pair of small breasts. Obtuse angled shoulders and a nose ring that gleamed in the artificial light. Janine opened her panicked eyes.

'Oh, Lori, it's you.'

'Morning.'

'Where's Mickey?'

'School.'

'Fuck, what's the time?'

'10.30.'

The clock on Janine's wall displayed 1:42. All three of its arms were immobile, stuck.

'Got a trial shift tonight at Riversweep.'

'Why? What happened to Black Truffle?'

'Left it. That asshole lost it at me last week. I was, like, ten minutes late. I told him to get fucked and walked out.'

'Great, another job you walked out of.'

'Well, what was I supposed to do? I don't want that negative shit in my life anymore.'

'Right.'

She forced Janine's black curtains apart. She beckoned the daylight in.

'Get up, I'll put coffee on.'

Janine sat up, her back facing Lori. Thin streaks of caked blood stretched with her back as she bent down to pick up her panties.

Steam rose up between the two sisters, from their coffee cups towards the dirty ceiling. Janine watched the raindrops, a red cushion clutched on her lap. Legs tucked under her body. Lori scrolled down her Instagram feed.

'What kind of dumb name is Riversweep?' She broke the silence after finding nothing interesting on Instagram. Janine broke her examination of the raindrops.

'Oh it's lovely, all girl crew. No bastard men on sight.'

Lori laughed.

'Men are just the worst.'

'You always say that. Surely you've met at least one good male recently?'

'No such thing.'

'Our Mickey's going to be a good man.'

'I try my best. But sometimes he looks at me so sad, I can't even deal.'

'He'll be ok.' Lori put her phone down and picked up her coffee. 'I'm going to Fiji for my birthday.'

'Oh. Amazing. When?'

'Friday. Me and Sam.'

'Wish I could go on a holiday.' Janine turned back to the raindrops. 'I haven't even been able to pay last month's rent. Can you help me out? I'll pay you back as soon as I get paid.'

'Are you kidding me? You don't even have a fucking job!'

'I'll get kicked out, it was due last week.' Janine's voice grew softer.

'Did he pay you maintenance last month?' She asked.

'He hasn't paid in months. He has no job. I don't even know where he is.'

'How do you think Mickey feels? His dad's a criminal. Mum's got no job.'

The rain turned torrential.

'I always told you he was useless. Mum told you. Dad told you.'

'Your dad, not mine. He locked me up in the house, remember?'

'He was right. Still you went and got knocked up by that piece of shit.'

The coffee was cold.

'You're the responsible one. I'm just a dumb bitch.'

'I'm off.'

Janine picked Mickey up after her trial at Riversweep. The rain had stopped. Lori didn't invite her in.

'Bye Lori,' Mickey said, with sad, wilting edges on his voice.

'Bye lovely.'

'Got the job, I'll pay you back soon,' Janine said, and scooted off.

Lori lit a joint. Her mind was full of thoughts of a sister who scratched her back till it bled. Who dealt with life by drowning herself in wine. And a nephew who always spoke with a sad voice.

Her grandma's words came to her, spoken so long ago, when Janine had returned home pregnant and sick. Lori had called her a dumb bitch. She'd said that she didn't want Janine in the same house as her. Grandma had told her to shut up.

'Family is who we go to when we have no one else to go to, that bond runs deeper than any other,' she had told Lori.

She logged into her bank account and transferred a grand and a half to Janine's name.

*Available Funds: $83.72*

She didn't do it for Janine. She did it for her Mickey. She couldn't bear the thought of him going to live with his wretched father.

She had come so close to her piña colada dreams.

'Finished packing yet, Lori?' her boss Sally asked over their late lunch the next day.

'Still a bit left.'

She hadn't packed anything. She hadn't even told Sam she didn't have enough money to go any more.

Every client that day had asked her how long she was going for. Or if she had been before. Or they reminisced about their own holidays.

'Well, go and finish it after lunch. No more appointments, I can finish early too. Just need to go to the bank.' She took some sachets out of the safe and placed it in a tote bag.

'I'm parked near the plaza,' Lori said.

'Me too, I'll walk with you.'

Sally's keys jingled with each footstep as they walked down the main street.

'We went to Fiji, it was '97, I think. Brett and me, when we were married. It was beautiful. Ten days we were there, no, thirteen, because of the cyclone. But that was February. It's not cyclone season now?'

'No.'

'Is everything OK?'

'Just worried about Janine.'

'She'll be fine. You deserve a break.'

Sally's phone rang, quite loudly.

'Hi Sally speaking … oh Mrs Johnston … oh my god, yes, yes, of course, I'll be there in five minutes, so sorry … yes see you there.'

She turned to Lori.

'Oh my god, I forgot Mrs Johnston moved her appointment! Can you drop this off?'

'Of course, go!'

'Sorry honey, see you in a week, be safe!'

The street was deserted. Through some damned coincidence, she found herself outside a travel agency. The poster on the display window told her to get her holiday *off to a flying start!*

The sun in Fiji wasn't as Lori had imagined it to be. It was hot and sticky. Uncomfortable. And there were mosquitoes—everywhere. She did get her piña coladas though. Served in green coconuts. Sam lay in the hammock next to hers, one sun-screened arm dangling loose, the other holding her own green coconut.

'Did your boss freak out about you going away?' Sam asked.

'She was a bit nervous. The temp seemed OK, though.'

'It's only six days. She'll be fine, right?'

'Yeah, she's had the salon for sixteen years.'

'Damn we're talking about work again.'

'I'm going to quit.'

'What? Lori?'

'Yep.'

'Why?'

'I wanna get away from Melbourne.'

'Where to?'

'My aunty has a salon in Morwell.'

Sam had hopped off her hammock and was standing next to Lori.

'But, it's such a good job, isn't it?' She said.

'Yeah, but time for a change I think.'

Lori's phone buzzed incessantly under her thigh. She knew it was her mum, she already had three missed calls from her.

'Well … cheers babe.'

They bumped their green coconuts together, and drank the last bits of their piña coladas.

'Another one?' Sam asked.

'Of course.'

She pulled out her phone after Sam went to the bar.

MUM

Missed Call!

1:23 PM

Missed Call!

1:25 PM

Missed Call!

2:05 PM

Missed Call!

3:20 PM

*Janine in hosp. Call me asap, Mum*

3:21 PM

She tucked her wild hair back in place. A mosquito landed on her arm and dug its proboscis in. It stabilised its skinny legs between her arm hairs and started sucking. So focused, it became oblivious to everything around it. Lori watched it fill up with her blood for a few seconds. Then she killed it with one swift strike and flicked it off.

Her phone buzzed again. "For fuck's sake," she muttered.

It wasn't from Mum.

SALLY WORK

*Lori, hun, bank saying last wks takings*
*not deposited. U dropped it off on thurs?*
*Sorry to bother u on your hol. Sal*

3:22 PM

She closed the message and leaned back into the hammock. The sun burned her eyelids.

'There you go hun,' Sam said, returning with two new coconuts. She took her fresh piña colada. Sam started telling her about a friend of a friend who worked at a salon in the city …

Lori stared at the waves, slowly rolling onto the beach and dissipating.

# 26

# Long Haul

## *Claire Orchard*

When I was a teenager, dreams involving my dead father
always entailed the romance of travel.

My subconscious must have decided that any possible heaven
was going to be far enough away

to need serious long distance transport options.
There was the dream about the ferry boat, the one about

the double-decker bus, another had him arriving on a paddle steamer
looking uncomfortable in his black wool overcoat,

one hand clinging to his briefcase as he perched
precariously on top of an enormous pile of bananas. That was

a pretty good one. But, in my categorical all-time favourite,
he arrived on a Boeing 747, through a canopy of clouds.

Sunlight reflected off the aircraft's white wings
as it banked towards the runway, momentarily blinding me. It landed,

taxied to the terminal, where the ground crew wheeled over the stairs,
the air crew flung open the door, and he emerged.

He stopped for a moment, poised on the top step. My father,
smiling down like a god. He was blocking the access way.

Loads of other dead people, people I didn't even know,
clustered impatiently at his back, pushing,

but he wouldn't budge, even though I was waving
like mad, to show him where I was.

# 27

# Making His Mark

*Charlotte Duff*

'I'm telling ya mate, it hit us in the guts as soon as we pulled the carpet back. This big.' Johnno put down his beer so he could hold out both his hands. 'He must have written it into the slab after he laid it.'

Russ laughed, tumbling the coins in his pocket as he eyed the barmaid. 'Like an artist.'

'But signing in secret, you know?' Johnno drained the last of his beer. 'The concrete woulda been covered up straight after.' Johnno snorted, remembering the look on the new owner's face when she'd first seen the name, scrawled deep across the concrete slab she was paying Johnno to grind and polish. 'Doubt he ever dreamed some rich bozo would wanna see the concrete.'

Russ was already counting his coins for the next round. 'Did you get it out?'

Johnno laughed, kept his smile turned on for Tracey as she delivered their beers across the bar. 'Most of it. The top of the S went pretty deep. You can still see a bit of it.'

'And what did the old duck think about that?'

'Nah, she was more worried I hadn't got into the corners enough.' The new owner had run her hand over the sweep of the S that was still visible. 'I think she liked it.'

'*Shane*. Legend.'

'Yeah.' Johnno could still see how the name had swirled over the concrete, sinking in, holding strong even as his grinder ran over it as many times as he could. Part of it would always be there, obvious now to anyone who walked into the newly painted room, a dinner party story for the new owner.

'Hey, Trace! You made your mind up yet where we're going on our first date?' Russ yelled across the length of the bar, always braver when Tracey was further away.

Tracey laughed as if this was Russ's first offer. 'You know my policy, Russ. No dating the patrons.'

Russ held a hand to his heart. 'Aw, Trace. Don't make me choose between you and my pub.'

Johnno snorted into his beer, ignoring Russ's antics, the look on Tracey's face. He and Russ drank at this pub most nights, always propped up on the same stools by the bar. The front bar was all fluoro lights and blue lino, often cold on top of the brightness. Most of the regulars kept to themselves, drinking slowly, counting their coins out just as slowly. Johnno saw his father in some of these regulars, the way they'd nod hello. The way they'd sip their beer like it had been blessed. But he'd never tell Russ any of this.

Russ slapped his glass down on the bar and some liquid sloshed out onto the already sodden bar mat. He was careless compared to the other locals. 'Well, gotta drain the lizard, as they say.'

Johnno tucked his hands beneath his legs as he shook his head. 'No-one says that, mate.' Russ just waved over his shoulder as he walked to the men's.

'So, Johnno, how was the funeral?' Johnno hadn't even realised Tracey was so close.

'Oh. Okay, I guess. My brother organised most of it. I dunno. Most people seemed to like it. Hanged around long enough afterwards to get pissed, anyway.' It's what Johnno's dad would have wanted. They all said that.

Tracey leaned in closer, different now Russ wasn't around. 'And how are you?'

'Fine, you know. It'd been coming for a while. Wasn't a surprise.'

'Well.' Tracey pushed herself away from the bar as one of the regulars finished his drink at the other end. 'Let me know if you want to talk about it.' She held up her hand against Johnno's scoff. 'You might at some point.' Johnno could see Tracey's gentleness, thought perhaps she was reaching out for him even as she walked away.

Johnno's dad, as he'd lain dying, hadn't been up for much talking. No deathbed gibber-jabber from old Bill. He'd said it had worn him out, just trying to keep up with conversations.

The door to the men's slammed and Johnno could hear Russ's heavy feet walking back. His hand was hard on Johnno's shoulder. 'Another beer, mate?' The day was still warm outside, the sun yet to set, but Johnno was ready to make a move.

'Not today, mate. See you tomorrow.' Russ looked surprised but didn't try to convince his mate to stay, giving Johnno a sloppy salute instead.

'I hope you find more names to grind into dust tomorrow, mate.'

After the service, the funeral parlour gave Johnno a DVD of the photos of his dad the family had pulled together. The photos captured Bill's growing ears and nose, the hairstyle that, essentially, stayed the same from when he turned 16 and got his first job at the real estate agency. Especially in the photos from the last 20 years, Bill was always holding a drink—beer, wine, port; he wasn't fussy. As long as he had a drink in his hand and friends around him, he said, he was happy. Johnno's dad couldn't understand why some people kept banging their heads against brick walls, trying to change people. 'Just leave it,' he'd say. 'Walk away. No point trying to row upstream in the dark.'

But Bill wasn't always easy to pin down. At times, he could also be a real bastard. Quick with a snide remark and a sneer when a son didn't measure up to his expectations of a man. But you don't include those sorts of comments in the eulogy.

Johnno walked home in the early summer warmth, still thinking about the thick letters he'd discovered in the concrete, the curve that had remained even after his grinding. *Shane.* He was a legend, just like Russ said. Johnno wished he could leave his mark somewhere, cut deep as if in concrete. All he did was expose a bit of the aggregate and then seal it up with a shiny polish.

He turned his face to the setting sun and decided he'd walk the long way home, past Tracey's house, even though he knew she was still working.

Johnno had found out where Tracey lived by accident. He was walking home from his dad's one evening towards the end, too late to catch Russ at the pub, when he realised she was walking ahead of him. She must have just finished her shift. She'd taken her hair out and she walked slowly, her body not as tightly coiled as it was at the pub, but he was sure it was her. He slowed his pace to hers without quite realising it, enjoying the sight of her hair catching the glow from the street lamp. The way her hair fell, sometimes providing a glimpse of the skin at the base of her neck, calmed him. She lived two blocks away from him, it turned out, and after she had turned the lock on her door and gone inside, it seemed natural to sit in the park opposite her house for a while, watching the lights go on and off as she moved around, the flicker of the TV.

He wanted to see the house now, bathed in soft yellow light, waiting patiently for Tracey's return.

Back at his small apartment, Johnno struggled with his front door, the bourbon from the pub's drive-through tucked under his arm so he could turn the key. He knew he should think about dinner but he didn't feel hungry yet. He turned on his laptop and sat in the gathering dark, letting the pictures of his father wash over him, trying to catch him. It was getting hard to see anything else in the room—the keyboard, his drink, the clock— but he didn't need to do anything for the pictures to keep coming. Bill and a mate messing around with a moose head. Bill, an early school-leaver, off to his first day of work, pulling at his tie. Bill sitting next to Johnno's mum, looking like he was there by accident. And then the later photos, parties and weddings. Bill wearing a battered Christmas-cracker hat that fell over one eye. Bill standing awkwardly in group shots, his hands in his pockets searching for car keys, leaving the group and already far away.

Johnno was only in a few of the photos, and never in one just with his dad. It was as if they both knew that building a bridge so they could come together, even for a photo, would only ever be a temporary, rickety thing.

The next day, Johnno stopped off at the pub after work as usual. The tables were already filling with the Friday business crowd, drawn by the drinks specials, but Russ's usual spot by the bar was vacant. Tracey waved over at him as he took a seat, already serving his beer. She smiled as she walked towards him, ponytail brushing her shoulders. 'You flying solo tonight, Johnno?'

'Looks like it. You haven't seen him then?'

'Not hide nor hair.'

'Just the one for now, I guess.' Johnno sipped from his beer amid the noise of the crowd, thinking about the bottle of bourbon back at his apartment. Tracey would be too busy to talk to him much anyway. She was off collecting glasses now from the crowded tables, laughing along with the office workers' attempts at humour. Johnno decided he could wait a bit longer for Russ.

Tracey stopped by his side when she returned, adding his empty glass to her stack. 'You ready for another one, Johnno?' It felt weird to have Tracey standing beside him on this side of the bar but also nice, as if they were out for a drink together.

'Course, Trace.' Johnno realised how much he was imitating Russ in his absence. 'It's Friday, isn't it?' Bill had loved his Friday night drinks, just like his father before him, lining up his glasses for the six o'clock swill before the bartender called last drinks.

'Still. Pace yourself.' Tracey smiled over her shoulder at Johnno as she walked back around the bar.

'Nah, no worries. I come from a long line of capable boozers.' Tracey laughed along with Johnno, but he wondered if he'd said too much. Then he saw how different her grin was now from the ones she gave out to her other customers, and he shrugged off his concern. He was nothing like his dad. He wasn't going to be reduced to a whisper by the end of his life.

As Tracey moved to serve another customer, Johnno sipped his beer more slowly. Once, years ago, Johnno had tried to confront his dad. It was late. Bill had been passing out at the kitchen table before he finally pulled himself upright enough to stumble down the hallway. At the last bump against the wall, Johnno, fifteen and already taller than his dad, yelled after him. 'Why do you do it, Dad? All the booze?' Bill had swung around, staggering a little as if walking tippy-toe over ice.

'You want to know why?' The bluster of bleary eyes and those enormous eyebrows drawn together. He'd taken a step towards Johnno, the rest of his body leaning off to the side, his head trying to correct it. But then he'd crumpled slightly, the shoulders gently sloping. His hand flapped. 'Argh.' And he'd turned back to the hallway, the soft shuffle to bed.

Johnno had left him to it, letting him creep further into the silence that was falling over the house, finding comfort and less shame there himself. He was left to chase the great revelation that had been about to burst out. That his father had married the wrong woman. His kid wasn't up to much. He always got a little less than what he asked for. These imaginings had made Johnno keep his head down, stay out of the spotlight for fear of highlighting all the areas he was lacking in, all the places he didn't quite make the mark.

And Johnno wondered whether the exhaustion that came from all this could get into your bones, into your genes, to be passed on to your kids. Make them tired before they'd even begun.

The photos weren't talking, and Johnno could never be sure. Perhaps his dad just loved to drink with a passion greater than anything else in his life.

Johnno nodded over at Tracey, accepting another beer even though she hadn't yet offered. She raised her eyebrows at him, the pub mostly empty around her, the office workers moved on, but started to pour it anyway. The sweep of her hand as she placed Johnno's drink in front of him, took away his empty, was like the curves of an S. 'Are you happy, Trace? This place, this job.' Johnno's loose arms waved around the dark room.

'I don't know, Johnno. It's a job, you know.' Tracey shrugged and leaned her elbows on the bar, tilting her body towards Johnno, who saw and then slowly looked away from how this pressed her breasts together.

'But are you getting anywhere with it?' His carefree, smiling dad was everywhere Johnno looked. 'My dad. You know, everyone said he was happy. He'd had a good life.' Johnno shook his head, the beer slowing his movements, closing in on this narrow focus. 'How could he be?' Johnno looked over the bar at Tracey. 'They didn't know him. He didn't do anything he coulda. None of it.' His mother raved about how his dad could have studied at university—literature, law, anything—was all set to sign up but got way-laid by easier options. Johnno had never been interested in study, had told himself when he left TAFE he'd never go back. And he knew his dad was a different kind of smart to him, the kind that could twist and destroy. But he'd had nothing to show for any of that. 'So what was the fucken point? How can you be happy with that?' Before Tracey could answer, start talking about family or perhaps a happy home, Russ burst into the empty pub, stumbling over the threshold, and Johnno sat himself straight, silencing his own gibber-jabber.

'Johnno! Mate! You're still here. Tracey, my good woman, a round of your finest whiskey.' And Tracey turned to Russ, her easy smile back in place.

'So, the cheap one you usually get, right?'

Johnno pulled out all the cash he had left. 'Come on, Trace. Just leave us the bottle.'

Johnno woke the next morning with a thumping head, the bench hard beneath him, his bones cold and aching. He was in the park opposite Tracey's house and he slowly realised he must have fallen asleep here waiting to see her come home, lock herself securely away. The heated shame made him feel woozy. All he could hope was that Tracey hadn't seen him, sleeping here like a bum. As the sun cracked open the horizon, Johnno walked home.

When Johnno woke up again he was on his couch, his head at a painful angle and the cricket playing softly on the television. He sat in his dark apartment, feeling revived after food and sleep. The sleeping pills he'd taken after eating had wiped him straight out but now it was like he had laser focus, and he realised he didn't fancy another night down the pub, fighting it out with Russ and his boasts, with the other punters for Tracey's attention. He thought of the way she would always catch his eye when he pushed open the pub's door, her smile jumping to fill her face. He needed to do something for her, something that would really impress her, make him be remembered. Like the curve that called out in the renovated lounge room, waiting for fingers to trail over it, stories to be told about it. He wasn't going to drift along like his dad, let life take him where it would.

He still had the hand grinder he'd used to get into the corners in the woman's lounge room after she'd complained. He could hook it up to the generator he used for outside work with no problems at all. He looked at his watch. Tracey would be on her usual Saturday shift into the evening and he had light for hours. Johnno sat on his couch a moment longer before running to grab his keys and then out his front door.

He was soon at Tracey's house, hooked up and ready to go. His work vest meant he wouldn't be troubled by anyone and he'd found the perfect spot: just at the start of her driveway and onto the footpath. She'd notice it straightaway. The straight line was easy, even with the circle of the grinder. And then a long, thick curve down that he swept the grinder over and over. It ended up crooked and a little sloppy. Not his best work, but a J etched deeply, undeniably there to stay. A point their story could start from.

No matter how long it took Tracey to make the connection, no matter what her decision was once she did, this mark of his love would be here forever.

# 28

# Trigger Questions

## *Joan Fleming*

As a child, my descriptions enjoyed reckless partiality.
I didn't know blood was a paste.
My teeth fell out and I was gifted money.
I learned to believe in Warlpiri as they lined the family hallway in
    picture frames.
I was sent home with pox and trigger questions.
*What kind of creature am I?*
I am the fat white bulb of the ghost moth.
I never enjoyed the scrambled taste.
As a child, I suffered the standard contagions.
In bed, I made my home report on the Australian insect.
*How do I live? What are my phases?*
I slept in a bed of generous and unearned proportions.
I gave myself the sailing feeling.
I recovered from a picture story of an emu who ends her own children
    with a rock.
Their bodies lined the family hallway in frames.
Ritual is a concentric circle. Dinnie, Hitler, Harry, Bullfrog.
I knew some of their white names.
I touched the dots til they rasped, then I went and watched television.
I practiced my routines in the living room.
I could be a darling of the world of white actors.
When my teeth fell out, I woke up with money.
I didn't know blood was a paste.

Witchetty grubs live in a burrow of their own creation.
I recovered somewhat, I returned to my learning.
Still a child creature reading the pictures.
Constructing world as a mesh that lets paste through.

# 29

# Love Letters Posing as an Epistolary Poem to my New Friend the Famous Poet

*Susan Bradley Smith*

## 1. Mad

Those photos. It had been one of the
organisational triumphs of my life to
create those albums of us, gloss and
matt, documents of the near and far
and seen and unseen. Unskilled and
frostbit from the scolding of your
goneness, I took them from the high
shelf and, watched by a stranger—
my new husband—I pulled every
second, every third, every fifth,
then every single panoramic lie
from its stuck place and cast them
upon the floor. Soon, I would try to
gather them and shark out their
histrionic demise, murder them,
replace them with ghosts from the
future. If I'd known what was to come,
would I have been so quick to trounce
history with melodrama? A bonfired
life, I say, explaining the past away.
Most disturbing: how pretty a pile
they made with their hypershine
and their denial of the grime of the

times that spun and twisted us into
tinsel. Auditioning for Christmas
baubles, they were.

Hang me.

*Dear ~~David~~,*

*I didn't know what to do. My first husband had been unhappy from the day he came to me in England. The first thing he did after arriving from Germany was lie down on my bedroom floor (I was sharing a house in Brompton with 4 girls, all of us freshly graduated and employed: me, a journalist; another, an Irish harpist for the London Symphony Orchestra; one beginning her Dutch diplomatic career; yet another, an engineer working on a highly mysterious project called The Chunnel; and my favourite, the podiatrist). He didn't really move for about a week. And on the eve of our wedding he slept outside in the car. We married young, at 21, and had 15 years of blitzkrieg fun, despite his melancholia making us a threesome. ~~I still miss him.~~ Love you.*

*Susie x*

## 2. Bad
These are the things that make me
foolish: basically, a long list that
spells 'unevolved'; and a shorter
one that sings 'fear'. Beyond
these accounts of failure there are
certain records of achievement
and (also) every so often, the world
does something crazy-good, like
supermoons or the evolutionary
frenzy of the northern lights and
who can argue with that kind of CV?
Blessings galore, yes, but (aside from
gratitude being a dullard's sport) last

night my husband came home late
and drunk and I felt like worn out
velvet. Who doesn't know by now
that before us stands yesterday?
Mostly, I felt a sure kind of stupidity.
I gripped my wedding ring, and
wondered at its weaponry, asking
myself softly if this was the best
metal I would know, all the time
wishing that you might kiss me
instead; buy me a pretty necklace
strong enough for strangling.

*Dear ~~David~~,*

*I never talk about my second marriage. I write about it, shamelessly, but conversation is too intimate a thing. Sometimes I conduct 'Short Talks on Brevity' trying to be honest but I largely lie. I blame precarious times for these rushed failures. I don't do anything thoroughly enough anymore, like protesting in the streets or flossing my teeth, or telling my friends anything that matters. It takes too long! When bad things happen I don't allow a proper soaking in disinfectant, I go for the swift wipe with an alcohol rub. Here's an example of briskness I admire from Emily Tennyson's grandmother: her complete diary entry for the day of her wedding, 20 May 1765: "Finished Antigone; married Bishop." Easier to opt for delayed damage than take pause. At least I read. More than I marry. Why am I telling you this? ~~Please write soon.~~*

*Susie x*

### 3. Ugly/Truth

There are some things you should know about
me before we take this relationship any further:
I like clothes. I believe in God. And I've killed.
They called me soldier so I am forgiven. My past
is top secret. But God is not my boyfriend. He

is the schoolyard bully of the perjured life, and
knows all kinds of things about trees and ropes.

I hang

my laundry, stringing it out against the sky like
a young wife flapping stiffly on a bed, wired
and pegged for her first ECT. I smoke, admiring
my clothes, their stripes, their polka dots, their
paisley shouts, their hopeful cleanliness, so much
brighter without me inside them. Stinging with
sunshine, I leave them to their morning.

Later

I will reinsert myself in them. I will take them
to Evensong, where I go each week to weep.
When we are wet, we need each other more
than ever. Afterwards, we'll go shopping, and
then my clothes will cling to me, fearful of my
certain infidelity. My thwarted faith. Tell God,
I will scream at them. Or someone who cares.

30

# Ribbons

## *Callum Methven*

The ribbons in her hair,
tied fatal flaws together, plumage
on the first day of school,
on the last day of the week,
the last day of the rift
between these two auspicious crests.
Clutching at these banks of fog
these ribbons robbing morning dew,
facetious thieves, these ribbons crying
shallow creeks between two locks of us.
Six or seven sirens screaming,
befallen to the calamities of them,
befallen to the brutality of little people
never ceases to astonish, never ceases
but the white cells have the final word.
She ties knots around the periphery,
around the absent dogma of these
hospital gowns, scarlet thread
interwoven with her flesh,
pale flesh fading faster
with this word, the final word
like ribbons in her hair.

Contributors

# Editors

**Bonnie Reid** is a doctoral candidate in Creative Writing at Monash University. Their research and poetry focuses on formal experimentations in trans* and genderqueer poetics. They previously co-edited *Verge*, 2016 and they are a co-creator of *Describe Series*, an occasional night of poetry and performance art held in their cousin's backyard.

**Aisling Smith** is a fiction writer who has had a number of short stories published in Melbourne, Toronto and Heidelberg. She is currently undertaking a PhD in literary studies, focusing on the works of David Foster Wallace. She is also co-editor-in-chief of *Colloquy: text, theory, critique.*

**Gavin Yates** is a doctoral candidate in Creative Writing at Monash University: his research interests include Surrealism, and Australian poetry. In 2014, Gavin completed his Honours degree, which was awarded the Jenny Strauss Prize for Best Creative Writing thesis. He is currently working on his first collection of poetry.

# Authors

**Ashvini Ahilan** has moved from UK, to Australia, for a year on a Study Abroad Exchange programme. She is currently in her third year of University, studying English Literature. Being a child of immigrants, she is particularly interested in issues surrounding Post-Colonialism.

**Aimee-Jane Anderson-O'Connor** is studying towards an Honours degree in English at the University of Waikato in New Zealand. Her work has appeared in *Starling, Mayhem, Brief, Poetry New Zealand, Landfall,* and *Tearaway Magazine* thanks to the tireless support of some of the best people on this great watery rock.

**Megan Blake** is a writer, photographer and previous editor of *Verge*; currently a doctoral candidate at Monash University in Melbourne. She is working (ferociously) on an argument about the competing justifications given to literary rules in 16C Neoclassical England, but took time out from that popular subject to write a submission for *Verge* because she really liked this year's theme.

**Susan Bradley Smith** is an award-winning writer, with research interests in Australian theatre and feminist cultural history. Her most recent book is the verse novel *The Screaming Middle*. Susan is the founder of the writing and wellbeing consultancy Milkwood Bibliotherapy; Artistic Director of Lennox Head Poetry Festival; and Senior Lecturer in Creative Writing at Curtin University.

**Natalie Briggs** is a poet currently living in Melbourne.

**Lauren Burridge** is a writer and literature student based in Melbourne. She's studying a Bachelor of Arts at Monash University, with a little Japanese on the side. She has had a few articles published online, and enjoys flavoured teas and well-meaning sarcasm.

**Brent Cantwell** is a New Zealand writer from Timaru, South Canterbury, who lives with his family in the hinterland of Queensland, Australia. He teaches high school English and has been writing for pleasure for 21 years. He has recently been published in *Sweet Mammalian*, *Turbine/Kapohau*, *Verity La*, *Brief*, *Blackmail Press*, *Landfall*, *London Grip* and in a New Zealand Poetry publication called *Penguin Days*.

**Killian Donohoe** lives in Melbourne. He completed his undergraduate studies at Monash University, and has been published in *Verge* twice previously.

**Charlotte Duff** is a writer and editor living in Melbourne. She is currently completing her first novel.

**Audrey El-Osta** is writing her thesis on the poetry of Dorothy Porter at Monash University. She yearns to one day live in a subterranean dwelling one could describe as a 'hobbit house.' Until then, you can find her skulking in libraries and bookshops, cackling like a cartoon witch over a meme.

**Joan Fleming** is the author of two books of poetry, *Failed Love Poems* (Victoria University Press, 2015) and *The Same as Yes* (VUP, 2011), and the chapbook *Two Dreams in Which Things Are Taken* (Duets, 2010). She currently lives in Melbourne where she is finishing her PhD in ethnopoetics, a project that has arisen out of family ties and ongoing relationships with Warlpiri people in Central Australia.

**Ann Jackson** is a freelance writer who haunts op shops, hoards stationery, and never stops talking about the time she performed with a rock band in Japan. She wishes her heart were as unbreakable as her Nokia.

**Jack Kelly** lives in Melbourne and is currently studying an Arts/Law double bachelor at Monash University. He can be found @__jack__kelly__.

**Allan Lake** is originally from Saskatchewan and has lived in Vancouver, Cape Breton Island, Ibiza, Perth (WA), Tasmania, Sicily and at present Melbourne. His collection, Sand in the Sole (2014) was launched at the Tasmanian Poetry Festival. In 2015 Lake won the Elwood Poetry Prize. During 2016 his poems appeared in Australian journals *Meniscus*, *Plumwood Mountain Journal*, *Poetica Christi* anthology and *Poetry Matters*.

**Callum Methven** is a twenty-two year old writer from Bunyip, Victoria, who isn't really sure if he should be calling himself a writer quite yet. He is currently patiently awaiting the launch of the James Webb telescope in 2018 and has recently returned from a semester's exchange in Colombia.

**T Venessa Nguyen** studies astrophysics and literature at Monash University. She lost her mind when the Higgs-Boson was confirmed, is learning to reconstruct her thoughts via writing, and in her spare time, cultivates a haphazard life philosophy. More as this develops on: http://www.venessa.co

**Claire Orchard**'s poetry has appeared in various journals including *Landfall*, *Sport*, *Sweet Mammalian* and *Best New Zealand Poems*. Her first collection of poetry, *Cold Water Cure*, was published by Victoria University Press in 2016. claireorchardpoet.com

**Chloe Riley** is an emerging writer from Melbourne, Victoria. She is a recent graduate from Monash University, having completed a Bachelor of Arts receiving First Class Honours in Creative Writing and a sub major in History. Chloe is currently taking a gap year and continues to write with intentions of pursuing postgraduate studies next year.

**Kerryn Salter** grew up in a small Victorian town (a 'dot on the map') before the internet. She looked forward to the fortnightly library van visits. She studied Creative Arts at VCA, before moving to Singapore 15 years ago.

**Sivashneel Sanjappa** is a Fijian-Indian writer based in Melbourne, who is currently writing a novel, and working as a chef. His stories are primarily inspired by experiences growing up in Fiji, and migrating to Australia as a young adult.

**Kim Waters** lives in Melbourne where she works part-time and studies visual art at LaTrobe College of Art. She has a Master of Arts degree in creative writing from Deakin University. Her poems have been published in *The Australian*, *Antithesis*, *Offset 16*, *Communion 5* and *Tincture*.

**Jena Woodhouse** held creative residencies at Camac Centre d'Art, Marnay-sur-Seine, France, and at the Australian Archaeological Institute at Athens, Greece in 2015. Her poems have twice been shortlisted (2013, 2015) for Canada's Montreal International Poetry Prize. She is the author/compiler/translator of seven published books.